Maid in Heaven

BOOK ONE OF THE *MAN MAID* SERIES

AURORA ALBA

Maid
in Heaven

Maid in Heaven:
Book one of the Man Maid Series.

Copyright © 2024 by Aurora Alba

Rusty Ogre Publishing
www.rustyogrepublishing.com

Casper, Wyoming, USA

All Rights Reserved.

No part of this book may be reproduced in any manner, or transmitted in any form or by any means, electronic, mechanical, photocopying, recording or otherwise, without express written permission by the author(s) and or publisher, except for the use of a brief quotation in a book review.

This book is a work of fiction. Names, characters, places, events, organizations and incidents are either part of the author's imagination or are used fictitiously.

Any resemblance to actual persons, living or dead, or actual events is purely coincidental.

Cover Art by Erica Summers

ISBN: 9781962854061

For Rick.

Thank you for showing me a love with enough adventures for a million romance novels.

Never forget how much I love you.

Content Warning:

This novel contains profanity, discussions of drug abuse, & sexually graphic descriptions.

|

"No, no, no!" Ava shouted.

"Oh, yes, yes, yes!" echoed the voice seeping from Ava's cell phone.

"*Please* tell me you're joking!" Ava barked.

Her friend hysterically laughed on the other end. "It's not a joke. He's coming over."

"Oh, for the love of... Madison! Why would you do that? This is, like, the worst day for that. I have a video call with a chairman from London this morning!"

"Well, tell him to start in the bathroom or something."

"You paid some stranger to come into *my* house and clean it? Without my permission? That's so... *rude*."

"He's not a *stranger*. I've known him since high school! He's a good guy and a hell of a maid."

"By the way... a maid? In Jackson Hole?" Ava's lips raced as she spewed her protest frantically. "This is friggin' Wyoming. I mean, I knew the billionaires were kickin' the *millionaires* out, but is that even a *job* anymore? *Maid?* Is that even the politically correct term?"

"Slow down. You're doing that thing where you talk at the speed of sound. You're spinnin' out. Take a breath. He calls *himself* a maid, so I'd say you're safe on this one."

Deflated, Ava sunk into her La-Z-Boy, one left behind by her ex-husband when he moved out months ago. "Madison, I'm gonna send him home."

"No, you're not! You're going to let him clean up your pigsty of a house. I'm tired of coming over there and moving the laundry off the couch just to find a damned place to sit. You're out of control. This first one's on me. It's my *gift* to you."

"Daniel was the neat freak," Ava growled. His name made her heart pang with sadness and his posture slump with embarrassment. "Now that he's gone, what's the point in keeping a spotless place?"

"It's time you get your house… and your *pipes*… cleaned," Madison joked.

"Oh, fuck off. Nobody says that anymore. Your age is showing." Ava winced at the realization that there was no getting out of this. "*Fine*, but he keeps his clothes *on*. I don't need these Brits to think I'm some sort of dominatrix or something." Ava shook her head silently. "I have to go. Catch you later."

"I'll be waiting. Spare no detail. What he *wore*… how he *cleaned*… if you *banged* him," Madison teased.

"I'm hanging up now."

"*Wait!*"

"What?" Ava snapped, desperate to be off the phone with Madison, who sounded like a hyena with all the constant cackling.

"Do you have condoms? You know… in case?"

Ava pressed the *end call* button on her cell.

She *didn't* have condoms. She threw them out when she found out she couldn't have children.

The divorce followed shortly after.

She was left with the house and Kuda, her Staffordshire Pit Bull terrier. His short snout and wiggly body brought her comfort in those dreary, lonesome months.

Trotting in from his doggy door, Kuda made his way through the dining room into the living area. He got a running start and hopped onto the couch, curling up on top of a pile of clean clothes that were folded but not yet put away.

The doorbell chimed.

Ava's heart jumped into her throat. Dreading the intrusion, she looked at the porch-cam notification on her phone. Selecting the alert, that's when she saw him…

A God among mere mortal men.

Her eyes nearly fell out of their sockets at the gorgeous male standing on her porch, muscular form bulging out of a Halloween-quality police officer costume. His face looked like it was chiseled from stone, with robust, angular features. His blue eyes peered into the lens. Muscular biceps jutted out from beneath the short sleeves of the faux uniform.

Ava glanced down, eyeing the bulge in his pants. *The man packs to the left,* she thought before chastising herself for the lurid leering.

She subconsciously twisted a piece of her shoulder-length red hair around her finger before pressing the microphone button to speak. "Hello?"

"Good afternoon, Mrs. Quinn—"

She tapped the microphone icon on her screen and spoke, "It's *Ms.* Quinn."

"I'm so sorry." His words were genuine. He ran a hand through his short frock of sandy-blonde hair. "So many of my clients have been married. I just assumed. I beg your pardon, ma'am."

"You know what they say about assuming things, right?"

"Yeah, it makes an *ass* outta *you* and *me*," he recited the dumb quip from memory. He locked his brilliant eyes onto the camera again. The masculine voice dribbled from his lips like honey. "Madison Miller hired me for a deep clean package. I'm your maid, Will Jessup."

Ava held down the mic button again. "May I ask why you are dressed like a *Reno 9-1-1* reject at eight thirty-two in the morning? It's freezing outside."

He simply chuckled.

The sound of his laugh made her weak in the knees.

"I grew up here. I'm used to the cold," he added with a million-dollar smile full of teeth as white as the snow behind him. "I'm pretty sure your neighbors are getting a free show. Maybe you could let me in so they have less to talk about?"

Damn. He was right!

Ava trudged to the door and yanked it open. She growled quietly. "*Fine. Come in.*"

"*Sure thing,*" Will whispered as he stepped over the threshold.

Once the door was shut, Kuda erupted into a symphony of ferocious barks, his display of anger betrayed by his wiggly rear and adorable pit bull smile. Will bent at the waist to greet him. The beefy animal raced toward the stranger, jumping on his hind legs to attack the man with eager kisses.

"Worst guard dog ever." Ava rolled her eyes.

"Dogs are better judges of character than we are. He knows I'm only here to help, don't ya buddy?" Will grabbed the tag on the wriggling pup's collar, read it, and snickered. "*Barry Kuda*? Clever."

"I just call him Kuda." Ava managed a smile.

Once the dog had his fill of ear scratches, Will glanced around. Ava followed his gaze, mortified by what he was seeing. Along with the clean clothes that had taken up residency on the couch, there were take-out containers cluttering the coffee table, pizza boxes, stacks of unread mail, dishes, paperwork, haphazard piles of movies, and stacks of paperbacks needing to go back in their respective spots in her bookcase. A thick layer of dust had taken up real estate on picture frames, along with the massive flat-screen television that hung on the wall opposite the couch.

"Wow, you have a party or somethin'?"

"*Or somethin',*" she said lowly, avoiding the subject. "Look, you don't have to clean. I'll tell Madison you did, and you can leave and keep whatever she paid you. It's nice of her to do this, but..." At a loss for words, she gestured to his costume, "I don't need this today."

"*Ms.* Quinn," he said, stressing her official title, "look, no disrespect intended, but I'm gonna have to send over someone in a *hazmat* suit if you don't let me clean because this place, no offense, is bordering on health hazard." Will swiped a finger across the dusty photo frame beside the front door. It featured a torn picture in which only Ava remained, broadly smiling in a flowing white gown and veil. He looked at his fingertips and then wiped them off on the tight black pants of his costume.

Ava frowned and crossed her arms in disappointment in front of her busty chest.

"Plus," he smiled, "if you tell your friends I cleaned your place, and it looks like *this* when they come over, I could lose a lot of business. My reputation is on the line, Ms. Quinn. I typically cater to wealthy, lonely women, and, *boy*, do they *talk*."

"I assure you, I'm just messy."

"Understood."

"Fine," she groaned, rolling her eyes.

"Fantastic." He grinned. "Now, this costume is part of my service. I warn all clients up-front that my service has the same rules as a gentleman's club: look but don't touch."

Ava felt a surge of heat at the thought of the Adonis in front of her, stripping down in the privacy of her home. Flustered, she looked away bashfully.

He smiled as if her reaction to him was as expected as the morning sunrise.

Ava stood straight. "So… Madison said she went to high school with you?"

"Yeah. We did."

The awkward silence between them mounted palpably for a moment. Finally, Ava spoke.

"Right. Well, I have a conference call via webcam here in a few minutes. I really need you to stay out of sight. So start with the bathroom or something.

"Can do. Anything else you need me to tackle today? Because this," he gestured to the house, "is going to be more than a one-time visit."

"Don't count on it. Like I said, I appreciate what Maddy was trying to do, but don't expect a call back. I'm not in the market for a maid."

Will scrunched his lips together, put his hands on his tactical belt full of fake plastic guns and furry handcuffs, and looked around. "Understood. Kuda and I are on it. Aren't we, Kuda?"

The pit bull stared at him, breathing hard.

"Ms. Quinn, we will whip this place into shape and stay out of your way. I will stay quiet as a mouse." He saluted her and headed down the hallway toward the kitchen and bathroom, assessing the dwelling. Padding behind him, Kuda happily followed his newfound companion into the kitchen. Will let loose a sarcastic whistle of disapproval. "Good Lord, what happened in here? Is that pot moving?"

Ava flattened her lips together, pinching her eyes closed. "Whatever happened to *quiet as a mouse?*"

"*Oh,* it's just a Brillo pad." He let out a sigh of relief. "It's fine. Disregard."

Ava shook her head and huffed, trying not to smile at the handsome stranger rooting through her home. She headed into her office, hurriedly twirled her auburn hair up, snatched a pencil from her desk, and wove it through the makeshift bun, pinning it against her head. Sitting down at her modern-style glass office desk, she sunk into her comfortable black leather office chair.

She awoke her computer and typed in the passcode: her old wedding anniversary.

She'd have to change that at some point…

She angled the camera at herself and realized that it would capture the mound of shredded photos and wedding gown lumped into a pile behind her. Her friends had taken turns wearing it with a black veil at her divorce party, which, of course, was Madison's idea.

Madison was right, though.

Getting rid of a cheater *was* grounds for celebration.

Ava picked up the heavy, silken garment and hurled it out of sight. She tossed the photos into a metal trashcan and returned to her chair. She pulled up the appointment link and double-clicked. The video-chat client opened up. Her thumbnail icon popped up first in the virtual conference room. Her pale skin looked ghastly in the unforgiving lens, and her freckles seemed more pronounced on camera. She cursed herself for not applying any makeup. Instead, she plastered on her most pleasant smile.

Donald Breckin, a balding man in his fifties, popped up on the larger screen. She couldn't help but think of Ben Franklin's iconic image. The resemblance was striking.

"Good morning, Ava! Thank you for meeting with me."

"Of course, Mr. Breckin. I apologize for not being able to grant you a longer window of time to talk, but as you know, we are in the middle of this merger, and there is no such thing as free time."

Donald Breckin chortled and wiped something from his keyboard. "No problem, hun. We can get straight down to brass tacks."

"Great. Mr. Breckin, I want you to know that I am here for you as your liaison, and I understand you have some questions for me."

"Yes. A couple, if that's alright."

"Absolutely. Fire away." She steepled her hands in front of her face and leaned in intently to listen to his concerns.

"I'm hearing rumors that your people are saying my wages are too high and that so many expenses need to be cut? The business side of my laboratory is operating *well* within normal limits. We aren't blowing money here haphazardly. I assure you, every expenditure is necessary. This laboratory needs to *raise* prices. Not *lower* them."

"I see," she said calmly. "I hear what you're saying. We don't fully know the ins and outs of how your business operates, but, Mr. Breckin, we've acquired several businesses like yours over the last decade and created a network of laboratories to handle more tailored needs. We keep costs low by doing bulk loads of samples from the individual hubs. We are acquiring you to make your lab a highly-specified and smooth-functioning hub as well. We are seeking high-volume, low-error results with quicker turnarounds. We feel your company is going to be a welcome addition to that. That said, we obviously have to stick to the overall financial strategy of cost-cutting wherever possible to keep expenditures across our entire network of labs low overall. Does that make sense?"

"Sure, but how will that affect my portion for the years we determined in the contract? Could we have been realizing more profit with—"

Don stopped and then squinted at his screen.

"—Is that… a *police officer*? Is everything alright? Are you in some kind of trouble?"

"What?" Ava snapped, spinning around in her chair.

Will Jessup stood in the doorway, waving apologetically in his police uniform, biceps bulging from beneath the tight fabric. "Sorry. Can I borrow you for a quick second?"

Ava squelched an internal scream and turned back to the camera. "Don, this is my… *cousin*. He thinks he's a police officer. He's *not well*. Would you please excuse me for a moment?"

"Certainly," Donald said, face frozen in a bemused expression.

Ava grabbed Will's arm and walked him back down the hall to the living room.

"Ow!" Will hissed. "You have a grip like a *gorilla*."

"I said no interruptions! What the *hell*?"

"I need cleaning supplies to tackle that kitchen."

"What?! What kind of maid doesn't have his own cleaning supplies?"

"Did you see me walk in with anything?" he asked sarcastically. "Rich women pay me to clean their homes. They provide the cleaning products. It's written on my website and on the contract."

"I didn't see your website!" Ava huffed. She looked around and rubbed her forehead anxiously. "Everything you need is under the kitchen sink. You know, where a *normal* person stores their cleaning products. Now, if you don't mind, I have to talk a man out of backing out of a multi-million-dollar deal. I need to *focus*. If I lose this client—"

"Yes, ma'am!"

His response only further infuriated the already frazzled Ava.

"Go!"

Will disappeared down the hall, handcuff chains jingling against his tight buns. Ava rechecked herself, straightening her pink pajama bottoms in an effort to salvage her image. As she feigned confidence, she strode back to her office and shut the door.

She gracefully took a seat. "So sorry for the interruption, Don."

"It's *Donald*," he corrected.

"Of course." She bit down hard, pretending to smile again. "My apologies. Now, I'm sure you have more questions, and I want to make certain that I answer all of them for you."

"I want to talk about my shares."

Ava knew it was coming. She clenched her hand into a fist beneath her desk. "Yes, you understandably seem as though you may have some reservations regarding the compensation."

"Your company seems to be all about the bottom line. A business like mine took a *lifetime* to build. It's my *legacy*."

"I understand that, Mr. Breckin—"

"Do you have children, Mrs. Quinn?"

"It's *Ms. Quinn,* actually." It had suddenly become painful for her to smile at the thought of her official title reverting. "And, no, I don't."

"Neither do I, Ms. Quinn. This company is all I have. I'm giving my baby to you, so to speak." Don sat back in his seat. It groaned beneath his weight.

Ava gripped the arms of her chair so hard she feared one might shear off, but her forced, pleasant smile washed across her face. "Well, you're not *giving* it to us. It's an eleven-million-dollar buyout. Your legacy will live on, and we will expand into all new territories with it. That said, if you have an issue with your compensation, I'm happy to discuss it further."

The words came out more curt than she had intended. His previous comment about children had knocked her off-kilter. Now, she was having difficulty righting herself again.

"It's not so much an *issue* as it is a generous offer to assist in these matters. I imagine a little lady like you would want to know if you're making a mistake or missing out on opportunities to make more money. And those additional profits would trickle down to what we'll call my *compensation*.

Eleven-and-a-half-million. You're set for life, you idiot.

She nodded casually. "Let me talk about that with the higher-ups and get back to you."

"Yeah, go ask the big dogs. I'm sure the other men will agree."

Ava felt rage bubble inside her and wanted to end the conversation as calmly as possible. "Well, Donald, as always, I appreciate any and all of your suggestions and am happy to field any more questions you have at a later date."

"I'll shoot over some ideas I've been having the last few nights that might help you all rob me blind even more." He chuckled insincerely.

"Well, I'll be looking forward to that email."

"Sounds good, doll."

"Is there anything else you'd like to discuss?" *Perhaps my failed marriage?*

"No, I think we are all set."

"Great." She felt relief wash over her. "Alright, Mr. Breckin, you take care."

"You too, hun."

Ava slammed her middle finger hard against the *end call* button, clamped her eyes shut, and shoved her face into her hands. After taking in a deep breath, she shouted, "Fucking *asshole*! Oh my *GOD*. What an *idiot!* It's *eleven million. Ugh! Dickhead.* It isn't worth *half*—"

Ava opened her eyes.

Don was staring at her in utter shock.

With her fraying nerves, she must not have hit the button right. The call had obviously *not* ended.

She swallowed hard, her voice barely escaping her lips. "Fuck."

2

The house was silent as a cemetery. Oblivious birds chirped, fleeing from the empty feeder outside Ava's home, casting avian-shaped shadows across the bleak shit show that was now her life. A south-bound flock of black-capped chickadees spattered a curved line of dung across the hood of her car, one which had not left the driveway in days.

There was no need. Where did she need to go? She was out of a job.

She had no *purpose*.

First, Daniel had quit on her. Then, her job of nearly eleven years tossed her to the curb, too. After losing the multi-million dollar Breckin Labs account, she was expeditiously dumped from the payroll and thrust back into the harsh world.

It was nearly a week later, and she had yet to motivate herself to get out of bed, save for the obligatory trudge to the bathroom. Crinkled cookie dough sleeves and empty ice cream tubs littered the floor of her disheveled bedroom.

With the blinds drawn, she closed her eyes, hoping some unseen force would come to take her out of this dumpster fire of her own making. Perhaps she could sleep it all away.

"Ava?!" a bellowing female's voice sounded through the stillness.

Kuda leaped up beside Ava on the bed and stood over her, ferociously barking at the intruder, hackles up.

"Ava?!"

The voice had come from *inside of her house*.

"Who's there?" she asked cautiously, sitting up from beneath the rumpled duvet covers. She scrambled and grabbed a spoon off the dresser, hoisting it into the air as if it would offer some semblance of protection. "Speak!"

"It's fuckin' *Santa Claus*. Who the hell do you *think* it is?" Madison said with an eye roll as all six feet of her strode through the cracked-open door casually. Her slender silhouette was barely visible in the darkened house, giving her unannounced presence an ominous feel. She looked like an angel of death, blonde and lanky, and for a split second, Ava hoped she'd come to put an end to this pathetic excuse of an existence once and for all.

Kuda quieted down. In full wiggle mode, he thrashed at the sight of Madison, jumping off the bed and running to her, nearly bowling her over with his muscular form.

Suddenly, the blinding overhead lights flicked on, LED ones Daniel had *insisted* on. The garish things were yet another painful reminder that he always got what he wanted.

"Gah!" Ava grunted, shielding her eyes from the light. The pale blue color of her walls now seemed far too bright. "Whyyyyy with the lights?"

"Jesus, Harla, you look like shit."

"Yeah, well, you look like Slenderman's illegitimate lovechild. And… stop callin' me Harla. You know I hate that. No one even gets the reference anymore." Ava flopped her face straight into her pillow with all the thrust she could muster.

"Why's it gotta be illegitimate? That's just unnecessarily hurtful," Madison said, kicking a paper tub that once contained vanilla bean like a soccer ball at the wall. It hit with an audible *thunk,* and she screamed. "GOOOOOOOOOOOOOOOOALLLLLLL!"

"Madison! Stop! For the love of God!" Ava's voice was muffled by the pillow.

"No way," Madison continued on, completely unfazed by Ava's protests, "now that you got your maiden name back, it's on like Donkey Kong."

"I didn't like it growing up, and I sure as hell don't like it now. I feel like I should have 'The Price of a Bride' tattooed on my forehead above Fabio's face when you call me that."

"Pfft, face tattoos are so 2005." Madison riffled through the makeup and brushes on Ava's vanity, leaned down to pet the needy pup following her through the room, and made her way over to the window.

"Why are you here?" Ava groaned.

Madison ripped the curtains open, suddenly whirling like a flaxen tornado of anger to glare at the mess that was Ava Quinn. "What the hell, Ava?! You scared the shit out of me! I've called your cell, like, ten thousand times. No text. No call back. No email. Nothing!" Her expression was etched with fury, lips pressed into a thin line. "I thought Will had your body parts shoved in his trunk or something! You can't do that to me. I was really worried!"

Ava could tell by the sound of Madison's shaky tone that she meant it. "I'm sorry." She plucked a dried piece of marshmallow from her duvet, trying to recall how long she'd been in bed with the remnants of her Rocky Road. "I was... busy."

"Wallowing in self-pity with ice cream and a vibrator? Yeah, I'll bet that really made it *impossible* to use your phone for two seconds, so your best friend wasn't freaking out."

"I said I was sorry," Ava muttered, knowing if the roles were reversed, she'd have been just as livid.

"So, I see that you are, in fact, in one piece and not in a well in someone's basement, putting the lotion on its skin so it doesn't get the hose again. That's good." She pulled a miniature-sized candy wrapper from the back of Ava's hair and handed the thin plastic to her, scissored between two fingers. "You look like hell. You look like one of the bird turds on your car, all pale and shitty."

"Maddy," Ava chastened, talking down to her like an elementary teacher would a naughty child, "you're saying mean stuff aloud again. That's an *inside thought.* Remember, we talked about those?"

"Fuck your inside thoughts. This is me. In case you somehow forgot in your Snickers-laden stupor, I cuss. I talk shit. I'm a kick-ass friend and one hell of a lay, according to the middle men's bathroom stall at O'Malley's. If you don't like me for what I am, then tell me to fuck off. Otherwise, suck it up. I happen to *give a shit* about my bestie when she falls off the face of the planet for a damn week."

"You're right." Ava sighed. "Thank you for checking on me. I'm sorry. I just don't want to deal with any of this. I just needed some time."

"Fine. Have you had enough time? Cause I got some shit to talk about." Madison folded her arms across her chest.

Ava nodded and sat up against her oak headboard, wincing as the frigid touch of the wood seeped through her thin, silk pajamas.

Madison waltzed over to the bed, whipped back the covers, and hopped in like an eager child. "So, *officer sexy*," she became animated with her hands, "you know, the maid? Will?"

"Yeah. What about him?" Ava asked, genuinely not having given him a second thought since he left her home. She'd been too preoccupied with being a *train wreck* the last couple of weeks.

"He asked about you when he came by to clean my baseboards the other day. Seemed worried about you. Said he knew you were under a lot of stress."

"Cleaning baseboards? That's a euphemism, right? I can't seem to keep up with all the lingo these days."

Madison laughed, "No. Not a euphemism. Some people clean their baseboards." She looked around, making a face at the mess throughout the room. Finally, her eyes made it back to Ava's.

"The dude's a good listener. A while back, he helped me through all my shit with Mark. Maybe he could do the same for you. He's like a therapist *and* a maid. Worst case scenario, he could make some organizational sense out of all of," Madison motioned to the whole room, "*this*."

"Seriously?" Ava self-consciously tucked a matted mess of hair behind her ear. "This isn't a *joke*. In the last few months, I've lost my marriage *and* my career. If there was a person who has earned the right to a nervous-fucking-breakdown, it's me."

"Huh, funny. My invite to the pity party must have gotten lost in the mail." Madison shook her head and moved to the edge of the bed, wrapping her hand around something sticky on the frame. "Ewwwww." Her eyes drifted down to the comforter, one with an ornate design of gold satin flourishes stitched across a sea of blue. "When was the last time you *washed* this?"

Ava gestured to herself. "Hygiene has not been a priority as of late." She wiggled down into the covers and pulled them over her head, growling through the thick fabric. "I love you, Maddy, but now is not the time for your particular brand of tough love. Now is a time for Cherry Garcia, heavy sobbing, and tragic black-and-white romances. So, if you don't mind," Ava flicked her hand as if to shoo Madison out the door.

Madison's shoulders drooped. She hated seeing her friend's life in turmoil. She felt powerless, having unloaded the only weapon in her arsenal: abrasive but genuine love.

"Fine. If you want to wallow, whatever." Madison stormed out of the room.

Ava waited to hear the bedroom door slam behind her, but the sound never came. Instead, she heard the soft peel of a breached seal followed by the sound of cardboard slapping onto the counter. Drawers opened and closed. Metal clinked. If Ava had any grit left, she would have gone to investigate. However, the greedy grip of her bed kept her rooted snugly in place.

Moments later, Madison reappeared, and Ava peeled back the covers to her nose. Her friend held a pint of ice cream with two half-buried spoons.

Without warning, Madison flopped herself into bed, cracking her noggin hard against the wooden headboard. She hissed in pain.

A laugh bubbled out of Ava, her first in days.

"Yeah, sure, find amusement in my pain." Madison grimaced comically. "You're *sick*."

"You okay? That sounded like it hurt."

"Don't. Just… don't." Madison held up a flat hand to Ava's face, "Now, where's the remote?"

Kuda jumped onto the bed and crawled toward them, scratching his belly across the duvet, hind legs limp. His chocolate-brown eyes glanced between both women and the frozen tub full of creamy dessert.

Ava searched the folds in the fabric, snatched the remote, and handed it to Madison. She navigated into one of the streaming apps on the flat screen.

"We don't have to talk. But you need to know I'm here, and *I* need to know you're safe. So just tell me what you wanna watch."

Silence.

"How about *Casablanca*?" Ava batted her eyelashes wildly like a hopeful child. Kuda whimpered and licked his lips in anticipation.

Madison found herself staring over at *two* sets of pleading eyes and scoffed. "Ugh, you and your old fart black-and-white movies. *Fine.* Whatever."

Ava laid her head on Madison's shoulder and sighed. "Thank you."

Madison leaned away and craned her neck to look at Ava. "You know you smell like hot dogs and ass, right? When was the last time you showered?"

3

Will carried a large mixing bowl brimming with popcorn to the living room and spoke in his best faux-British accent, "*'Ere you go, yo' majesty.*"

Starla's cobalt eyes lit up with excitement, and she let out a giddy giggle. Her crooked smile warmed his heart. "Thank you!"

Snatching the large container with her small hands, she nestled into her usual spot on the leather couch and wrapped herself in a princess-patterned throw.

A few stray pieces of popcorn tumbled to the floor only to be quickly vacuumed up by Gremlin, their portly pug. Her rotund body never seemed to impede her surprising speed and timing, especially when it came to fallen food.

'What are we watching tonight, Starla?" Will sat, wrapping an arm around her.

"I don't know yet."

"Pick something good," Will muttered, plucking up a few buttery kernels.

As Starla scrolled through the selections, she took a deep breath and looked at her father. "Papa, can I ask you a question?"

"Sure. Shoot," he said, lobbing popcorn into his smiling mouth.

"What's a *gigolo?*"

As the last syllable came out of her young mouth, Will choked. "*Excuse* me? Where did you learn that word?"

"Well," she turned her body toward him, "Samantha said that *her Mom said* that you're a gigolo."

Will cleared his throat. "A gigolo… is an adult word."

"Okay, but what is it?"

"It's," he thought long and hard about the next few words, "a… person who makes love with people… for money."

"Makes love?"

He knew this conversation had to happen one day. He just hoped it would have been *later…*

Like when Starla was in grad school.

"Remember when you asked me where babies come from?"

"Yeah, I'm still a little confused about that." She nodded, bobbing tendrils of her curly chestnut-colored hair with the movement.

"Well, we can talk about that more when you're a little older, okay? The important thing is I'm not a gigolo, honey. That's just what Samantha's Mommy *wishes* I was." Will could practically see the gears of his daughter's mind turning.

"Why?"

"Because nobody wants to make babies with her."

"She said that's why you dress funny when cleaning houses sometimes. Do you need to wear a costume to make babies?"

"No, sweetheart. You don't." He chuckled uncomfortably. "People pay me to clean their houses in those costumes because it's fun, and they think it's… um… *entertaining*. But there is no baby-making involved, I promise."

"Why would they say those things then?"

"Some people are so miserable that they have to make other people feel bad. Samantha's Mom is just a bi—"

He stopped himself.

" — A *bitter* lady. Just ignore Samantha, okay? Samantha's Mommy is just mad that she asked to," he swallowed hard, "um… try to make a baby with me. But, you see, I turned her down."

"Why?"

"Because I already have one." He booped her on the nose with his index finger.

"Dad! You got butter on me!" She wiped her freckled nose furiously.

The truth was Samantha's mother, Charlotte, was Will's first client. She had heard through Samantha about Starla's medical issues and frequent school absences. She invited Will over to help out around her home and lawn for some extra cash.

One day, while her husband was away on business, she offered Will triple to do the work dressed as a scantily-clad cowboy, a somewhat masturbatory fantasy she'd confessed to having had for decades.

With a pile of bills from Jackson General Hospital and the cost of Starla's new port and insulin, Will wasn't in a position to turn the money down.

With a promise to keep quiet about the tawdry activities and to keep her hands to herself, he agreed to do lawn work and furniture assembly in the ten-gallon hat, boxers, and ass-less chaps she'd provided.

While her diamond-adorned hands never strayed from the pockets of her crochet romper, Charlotte hadn't kept the first half of her promise. Fortunately for him, she blabbed to a gathering of her closest female friends at their next weekly book club.

Will started receiving calls from a bevy of horny housewives in the Jackson Hole area with similar offers. Within a month, he found himself rotating through a roster of opulent homes dressed in whatever costume the owner requested.

He quickly ditched the lawn work due to its lack of discretion and offered a variety of private services within the homes, executing tasks from dusting in fatigues and dog tags to cleaning dishes in scrub bottoms and a stethoscope to assembling furniture in a headband and leather jacket (a favorite among the middle-aged die-hard George Michael fans).

The costumed cleaning cost extra but soon became an honest way to earn enough dough to get the bills out of collections. Six months later, Will was able to put the minimum down payment on the modest home where he and Starla lived now.

He recalled the uncomfortable exchange with Charlotte the last time he'd seen her. She'd traipsed downstairs in a red, see-through nightgown while Will was brushing grime from the grout on her tiled kitchen island in a Trojan soldier uniform. Behind him, she slid a hand into his painted-on gold shorts and rudely helped herself to a fistful of flaccid dick.

He jerked away in repulsed horror and fired her as a client on the spot.

Spurned and vengeful, Charlotte spent the following week telling anyone in her social circle who'd listen that he'd made a pass at *her*.

Thankfully, that rumor backfired and only seemed to invite more business.

The allegations made his client list double in no time.

Will questioned the new career choice long before the groping, lonely mother trampled his boundaries. Having his clients fawn over him was flattering, sure, but it felt like only a small leap from costumed cleaner to prostitute. It was a leap he was not willing to make for any amount.

He knew one day when she was old enough, he would have to answer to his daughter about it all.

Thankfully, today was not the day.

"Here." Starla handed over the remote and sighed like she'd just worked a double shift. "I don't know what to choose. Too many options."

Will laughed. For a six-year-old, sometimes Starla sounded like a full-blown adult. It never failed to make him laugh.

"I got just the thing."

"What?"

"I'll show you a classic tonight. It's black and white but bear with me. I think you'll like it."

"Nooooooo! Papa, those movies are so *boring!*"

"They're not boring, they're *art*."

"They kiss and stuff." She stuffed her mouth full of popcorn and spoke again as she crunched. "It's gross!"

"Love isn't gross. You wouldn't even be here without love," he added, pulling her in for a side hug. Gremlin jumped up on the couch beside them. "Plus, I love *you*, and *that's* cool, right? That's not gross. I love *Gremlin* here and—"

Before Will had time to finish, Gremlin buried her short face in the bowl of popcorn.

"*No, no, no!*"

By the time Will pulled her back, Gremlin looked like an overgrown hamster, cheeks puffy and stuffed to the brim.

"*Bad Gremlin!*"

Starla laughed as her father plucked up the voracious pug and plopped her back on the floor. Gremlin raised her front paw and batted his calf as if to plead for more.

"*Take your stinking paws off me, you damned dirty ape*," Will growled playfully. He grimaced at the slobbered bowl in his daughter's hands. Will took it, strode through the living room, pressed the lever on the trash can with a barefoot, and dumped the bowl's contents. "Probably got Gremlin goober on it now."

He started another bag popping in the microwave and then stuck his head out into the living room. "Soon as this is done, you ready to give this movie a shot?"

Starla dramatically deflated against the back of the couch. "What's it about?"

Will suddenly wondered if he's shown her *Gone With the Wind* too many times already. The kid was already picking up some of Scarlet O'Hara's over-the-top mannerisms. "It's about a cafe owner who has to decide whether or not to help his ex-girlfriend and her husband escape the nazis."

"What's a nazi?" Her small face stared up at him.

Shit. "Um, nazis are bad guys from the Second World War. They killed about six million Jewish people."

"Woah." Her eyes bulged. "Are they still around?"

"No." His head bobbled a little. "I mean, I guess it depends on who you ask, but the war has been over for a while, and everything is fine… *ish*… now."

"Oh. Okay." She flicked a stray piece of popcorn off her lap and delighted in Gremlin's intense hunt for it. Finally, the dog found it, scarfed the piece up, and eagerly licked the ghostly remnants of butter from the floorboard where she'd found it.

"Sounds a bit… boring."

"Aww, come on. Give it a shot. It's one of my all-time *favorites*."

"Ugh…. *fine*."

Relieved the barrage of questions had fizzled, Will returned with the fresh popcorn, popped the DVD in the player, and settled back in.

"Cas-a-blay-an-ka?"

"*Casablanca*." He smiled. "You're gonna love it."

***

Twenty minutes in, Starla was asleep, snuggled in her father's warm embrace. He stroked her hair as the plot of the romance unfolded before his eyes. It was as if he were seeing it for the first time. The movie had stirred emotions he'd not felt in the better half of a decade.

Passion.

Companionship.

Love.

The movies always made it seem so easy…

Boy meets girl. Boy marries girl. Boy and girl have a baby and live happily ever after.

His life, however, had been *anything* but a fairy tale. His was more like *boy meets girl. Boy and girl have a baby. Girl discovers drugs. Girl leaves boy and baby for her dealer…*

Starla was his life now.

He cherished all that he had but longed to have someone with whom to share it. He was stumbling through life with a daughter, one painful learning curve at a time.

Will scooped up Starla and carried her to her ballerina-themed bedroom, walls the color of Pepto Bismol. He laid her down and swiped her bangs from her cherubic face. He'd nearly made it back to the door when Starla stirred.

"Papa?" she cooed.

"Yeah?"

"You gotta do it like a burrito."

He laughed, understanding what it meant. He returned to her side, tucking the covers atop her in snugly on both sides until she was encased in a snug wrap.

"Thank you," she muttered with a yawn, extremities tucked in tightly to her sides as if rolled in a soft tortilla shell.

"You're welcome. I love you. Get some sleep."

"Love you, too." She blew him a comically loud kiss, and Will left the room, leaving the door ajar.

Walking back down the hallway to the living room, he was struck by the wall of lonely, almost deafening silence. He settled back into the couch and pressed play on the remote. As the classic film roared back to life, he glanced at the precariously-balanced stack of films on the TV stand. Every tale full of romance and new adventure. People taking risks, baring their souls, clutching on to old love letters, seeking out a soulmate in a single glass slipper, holding boomboxes on suburban streets, and chasing moving trains all in the name of love.

Will wondered if he would ever find a love worth fighting for. A woman who completed him. A romance John Hughes would pounce at the chance at the movie rights.

As Casablanca droned on, he fed Gremlin a handful of cold popcorn and tried to shake the gnawing and pointless notions from his mind. Who was he kidding? He was no prince with a castle waiting to sweep a beautiful redhead off her feet.

He was just a shirtless Cinderella, scrubbing floors in off-season Halloween outfits to afford insulin and a mortgage on a two-bedroom house with a crumbling back porch.

4

Ava's curtains yanked open. Sunlight flashed into the room, blinding her. Batting her eyes furiously, she finally made out a shape.

"Get up, Dingus. We're going to the gym."

"The hell I am," Ava groaned as she rolled over.

"Oh, yes, you are," Madison growled, grabbing Ava's bare feet. "Are you gonna *walk* there, or am I gonna have to *drag* your ass there?"

"There's no way out of this, right?" Ava asked, rubbing sleep from her eyes, desperate to focus.

"I mean, nothing short of assault."

"I'm not putting on makeup. You get me *au natural* or not at all."

"You can go in boxers and a *sombrero* for all I care, as long as you get your flat ass moving."

"Fine!" Ava tossed back the blanket and stormed toward the *en suite* bathroom. "By the way, I hate you."

Madison chewed her hangnail, gnawing it like a rodent. "You'll hate me more if you don't hurry the hell up."

***

The duo wove their way through gym equipment. The scent of sweat, body odor, and bleach stung Ava's nostrils. She trailed behind Madison with a look of disinterest mixed with mild disgust. The bright overhead lights made the dark circles under her eyes pop, and her rat's nest of auburn hair was held in an untidy ponytail with a lavender Scrunchie. A purple sports bra hung out from the stretched collar of her sweatshirt, which read: *Not today, Satan.*

Large aquarium-like windows framed the perfect scene of Jackson Hole just beyond the treadmill-filled cardio area. Late morning sun glinted across rolling hills, illuminating the landscape like something from a postcard. The gargantuan mountains in the distance, ones Jackson Hole was so notorious for, were dusted with freshly fallen snow beckoning skiers, summoning snowmobile owners, and granting steady work to the ever-ready plows that hibernated in sheds during the warmer months.

Madison spotted the leg press beyond a gathering of gym rats, all engulfed in deep conversation. She signaled for Ava to follow.

Ava didn't budge.

Madison slammed a fist into the hip of her painfully bright, lime-green yoga pants. Most of her outfits were the colors of the highlighter spectrum, bold and visually irritating, and this ensemble was no exception. "So help me God, part of my workout can be dragging your ass from machine to machine if I have to."

"Ugh!" Ava's shoulders slumped. She looked around self-consciously at the undulating sea of spandex around her.

Madison slapped her hard on the ass, sprinting ahead of her, beating her to the machine without competition. Clad in a neon green sports bra and hot-pink mesh tank, she patted one of the machines, signaling for Ava to take a seat.

"We're getting you back on the dating scene. If you're at rock bottom, then, by *God*, you could at least have a *rock-hard bottom*."

"You have such a way with words." Ava laughed, begrudgingly taking a seat on the leg press.

"You need to get *laid*. How long's it been?"

"It's been… a *while*," Ava mumbled, her cheeks blushing with embarrassment.

"What's 'a while?'" Madison asked with an arch of an eyebrow.

"I don't know," Ava mumbled, giving an awkward nod to one of the muscle-bound attractive men who walked past. "Over a year-and-a-half maybe."

"Wait. I thought you and Dan only divorced a few months ago."

"We did. But the months before that, he just was never, you know, *in the mood*." She shook her head and chuckled. "Well, turned out he *was* in the mood, just not with *me*."

Saying the words felt like a punch to the stomach.

"We'll get you through this shit. It sucks. You know I've been where you are. That's why I'm not gonna let you get away with anything." Madison grabbed Ava's legs and put them into place. "Now, you're going to act like you give a damn and do some fucking leg presses."

"Fine, ten presses, and we go home," Ava grumbled.

"No. Let's try *fifty*, and then I'll take it easy on you at the next machine."

"How about *fifteen*, and I don't lose my *shit* on you?"

"Thirty."

"Fine. Deal. Twenty it is." Slowly, a smile crept onto Ava's face.

Madison stacked some small weights on the machine. Meanwhile, Ava took a look around.

That's when she spotted him.

Those electric-blue eyes. The ones that seemed to bore right through her.

They were staring now, crinkled in the corners above that knee-weakening grin across his stubbled face.

It was the maid.

What was his name?

Will?

He removed one of his earbuds and walked toward them. "Hey! Remember me?"

An intoxicating mix of weat and spiced cologne wafted by her. Though part of her melted into jelly, her insides turned into a sudden jumble of nerves.

"Yeah, you're the guy who saw me get fired," she chuckled, though it wasn't funny.

"Yeah, about that, I feel like a good bit of that might have been my fault. I hope you know that it wasn't my intention to distract or frustrate you. In retrospect, it was just really bad timing. I should've just come back another time. I'm sorry for how all that went down and any part I played in it."

She smirked. "Mmmm. I appreciate that."

Madison wrapped her arm around Will and asked, "How's Starla?"

"She's good! Before long, she's going to be a force to be reckoned with, you can tell. Kids are still pickin' on her, but her comebacks are gettin' quicker and funnier every day."

Ava's eyes met Will's, and for a second, she felt dumbstruck. Quickly regaining her composure, she smiled, "It's nice to see you, Will."

"Yeah, nice to see you, too. You ladies have a good workout."

"No such thing," Ava fired back, followed by a laugh.

Will laughed and shook his head, returning the earbud to his ear and walking back to the lateral pull-down bar several yards away. Madison looked from Ava to Will, then back to Ava.

"What?"

"You should *bang* him," Madison whispered loud enough for those around them to stop and stare. "You can totally tell there is something there."

"Shhhhh!" Ava was mortified. "Shut the hell up. Everyone can hear you."

"No, he's got earbuds in. Look, Ava, from what I have heard, he gets around, and he's a damn good lay. Look at him. He's a single D.I.L.F."

"A what?"

"Oh Lord, you are rustier than I thought." Madison leaned in. "*Dad, I'd Like to F —*"

"I got it," Ava interrupted.

"So… Go ask him out!"

"*Him?!*" Ava was in shock. "Naw! I don't know if I'm ready. I'm bringing all of this," she waved from her unkempt hair to her dingy shorts, "nonsense into a new relationship. That's not fair to anyone. I need to get my life straightened out first."

In a display of uncharacteristic seriousness, Madison said lowly, "Life is messy. You deserve to move on. I'm not saying you have to *marry* him. Just… maybe go have a drink? You gotta get out of that house and go do something."

"I hear you… but, no, I can't do that. I'm not ready."

Madison placed her hand on Ava's arm, "Sack up, girly. You got this. Go."

Ava knew she'd have to listen to Madison goad her the whole time if she didn't. She was nothing if not annoyingly persistent.

"Fine. I'll go ask, but once he shoots me down, I'm only doing ten leg presses."

"Whatever. Deal."

The bargain had been struck. Now, Ava felt a flush rise from her neck through her cheeks. She stood from the press and walked toward Will. He was seated, tugging on the pull-down bar. She hesitated, studying his rock-hard body in the wall of mirrors before finally tapping him on the shoulder. He set down his weights and turned to face her.

"Oh, hey! What's up?" he asked, removing his earbud again.

"Thanks for what you said back there. We kinda got off on the wrong foot."

"Nah, you were just busy. I didn't take any offense."

"Thanks." Ava's heart pattered her chest like a drummer at a rock concert.

Will nodded and held eye contact with her for a beat.

"Maybe we should start this over. You know, clean slate. Ava Quinn." She stuck out her hand. "I'm an unemployed dog mom who abhors working out. Or, in simpler terms, a real catch," she joked, feeling beads of sweat form on the nape of her neck.

Will stifled a laugh and held out his hand. "Will Jessup. I dress up in too-small Halloween costumes and scrub the mildew out of rich people's showers."

She laughed aloud as they shook and then clasped a hand over her mouth before she could do something embarrassing like snort. She wasn't sure what it was about him. For a woman who regularly stood in front of large groups of men, gave training demonstrations, and guest lectured at symposiums all around the country, she suddenly felt tongue-tied.

"Would you," her lips twitched as she decided whether or not to finish the question, "like to grab a drink sometime?"

"I'm sorry." He sighed, chiseled face serious. "I have a rule. I don't date clients." His eyes showed how pained he felt uttering the words.

"No sweat. Doesn't hurt to ask." Her shoulders slumped with a mix of defeat and relief. At least the deed was done. Even if she'd gotten the answer she expected. "Although, for the record, *technically*, I'm not your client. Madison hired you."

"Gettin' off on a technicality, huh?" He grinned.

Ava felt her knees start to buckle and tried to force away the smirk forming on her lips.

Finally, Will spoke again. "You have a dog, right? What's his name again?"

"Kuda."

"Oh, yes," he snickered, "that's right. Barry-Kuda." He wagged a finger at her. "That's punny."

"I try." She shrugged playfully.

Will found his eyes settling on the spandex pattern practically painted on her shapely legs.

"Well, I suppose I don't see the harm." He rose from the bench and stepped closer, leaning a glistening arm against the back of the machine next to her. She felt tugged into some sort of gravitational pull, powerless to pry herself away from him even if she wanted to.

Ava looked around nervously, anxious to break his gaze.

"Do you know where Morad Park is," he finally asked.

With his body this close, she could feel his warmth radiating through her clothes like a space heater, penetrating her skin and warming her to the core. She watched a bead of sweat run down the side of Will's neck, traveling down onto his chest. She subconsciously bit her lip. Something about a sweaty man made her want to make him even *more* sweaty.

It was there.

She felt it.

The spark.

"I think so. That's the place on 12th, right?"

"Yep. It's the dog-friendly walking path around the river. Ever been?

"No, actually, I haven't."

"Good." Will smiled and leaned ever-so-slightly closer. "I can pop your cherry, then."

Suddenly, Ava's cheeks felt like they were being roasted with a torch at the comment.

Uh... say what?

"You free tomorrow?" He toweled his biceps and shoulders, bulging from the fierce workout.

Ava never wanted to be a piece of cloth so much in her *life*.

"Y-yeah," she stuttered. "Let me just check my work sched... ha-ha, just kidding, I'm totally free, like, *indefinitely*." Ava felt like a mess, stumbling over her words and joking about being unemployed. She felt hyper-aware of the nervous butterflies... no, *raptors*... clawing at her stomach.

"Great. Meet you there at one o'clock? I always take Gremlin there after lunch on days I'm off."

"Gremlin. *Cute*. I like the name."

"Great." Will stood straight and smiled.

Ava weakened at the sight of his perfect teeth. "Y-yeah. See you then." She turned, tripped on her own feet, and caught herself on an outstretched arm just before she fell.

Will had reflexively grabbed her. "You good?"

"Yeah, I, uh... clumsy feet." His touch sent a chill up her spine. "Thanks."

"Don't mention it."

"Don't worry, I won't. I'd like to completely scrub that from my internal hard drive. That's what I get for drinking martinis right before I hit the gym."

He stared at her for a moment, trying to decide whether she was serious or not.

"I'm kidding, Will."

Will looked relieved.

"Stone-cold sober. Just a klutz. Honestly, I'm fine."

Ava turned away, eyes bulging at Madison across the gym with a look of pure mortification.

Once she was a foot away, she whispered, wondering if she might puke right there in public. She clutched Madison's hands. "Oh, *God*, Maddy, what did I just *do*? I don't even remember what I *said*!"

"...And you tripped, you graceful little ballerina."

"And I tripped!" Ava pinched the bridge of her nose and scrunched her eyes closed.

"It's fine. He seemed unfazed." Madison grabbed Ava's shoulders. "Hey. Bitch. You're a hottie. Don't beat yourself up over one little rejection. You're smart and a hard worker. *You're a catch*. Stop acting like *prey* and be the fucking *lion*."

"You're right. I… got this," Ava repeated softly.

"What the fuck was that? Try again."

"I *got this*." This time, with more conviction.

"Give it more balls."

"*I... got... this!*" Ava growled.

"You're damn *right,* you do. Now start *acting* like it!"

Ava's eyes widened into two huge moss-green orbs. "*Oh!*"

Madison chuckled. "You look like you just got *electrocuted*."

"Maddy, he didn't turn me down."

"What?"

"He didn't turn me down. We are meeting tomorrow at some park."

"Alright!" She high-fived Ava and watched Will make his way into the locker room. Madison's head snapped back comically. "Girl, get on that machine this instant. We gotta get that ass *toned* so it can get *pounded*."

"Good *Lord,* you are foul," Ava laughed.

5

Furious Wyoming winds whipped powdery snow across the hood of Will's maroon truck like an aimless apparition. Towering mountains surrounded Jackson Hole, clutching the town in its frigid embrace.

Will idled at the curb, bolstering himself up in silence. The gargantuan estate was sprawling, with two stories and a huge wrap-around porch. With feathery clouds streaking the expansive sky, the client's looming home looked like something straight off of a Thomas Kinkade print.

A cottontail took off across a white dune. Will's eyes followed the rabbit as it darted through the multi-million-dollar property toward a neighboring home.

Down the road, a buck and his harem were nestled together beneath a mature chokecherry tree, somewhat sheltering them from the elements.

But as he surveyed, Will realized he hadn't yet spotted the *predator*.

Lurking, fierce eyes locked on him.

Prowling cougars were common here in the Rocky Mountains, but this was one he'd had tangled with twice a month for the last year...

Denise-fucking-Kronin.

He let out a deep sigh that fogged the windows, adjusted his outfit, and rolled his shoulders back.

Denise stood inside the glass front door, waiting impatiently in a skin-tight green sweater dress. Bottle-blonde curls flowed around a face that, thanks to her pricey plastic surgeon, strangely looked youthful from his aging Dodge Ram. The woman, petite and in her early sixties, flashed a veneer-laden smile and curled her finger seductively to coax him in.

Will smiled back at the long-term client and jumped down into the snow. His combat boots burrowed into the white powder with a loud crunch. He tucked his tight, tan t-shirt into his desert camo fatigue pants, dog tags clattering loudly together. Crunching his way up the steps in the frigid squall, Will made his way into the lion's den.

"Morning, Denise." He nervously double-checked the Velcro name tag on the chest of his camouflage jacket that read "Sgt. Sexy" to ensure it hadn't fallen off again.

"Good morning, handsome." Denise was already stripping off his camo jacket to expose the tight shirt beneath. Once it had been shed, she stood back and smiled, drinking him in. "You sure do know how to fill out any outfit I want."

Will flashed an appreciative smile, even though her objectification made him feel unsettled.

"Turn around. Let's see the back."

Will quickly wiped his feet on the welcome mat and did a slow spin in the middle of the checkered marble foyer floor. Denise clapped.

"I'm glad you like it."

"No. I don't like it. I *love* it. You make me want to send a rather generous donation to our troops."

He opened the coat closet and hung his camo jacket on one of the ornate hangers. Everything in her mansion was fanciful and adorned with gold flourishes, ivory, or marble.

"So? Will. Do you *notice* anything?"

Though he would never initiate a comment about such a thing, Will had, in fact, noticed how her once-average natural breasts had suddenly ballooned into weighty D-cups that threatened to topple her otherwise scrawny frame.

"You did something to your hair," Will teased.

"You know damn well I wouldn't mess with *perfection*. Keep guessing..." Denise gestured to her chest.

"Oh! They're… lovely." Will didn't know what the right answer was. The woman looked like a toothpick with two large, green olives stabbed onto it.

"They're nice, right?"

"Sure!" Will swallowed hard.

"Doctor Spatz is a genius. He's like *Michelangelo,* and I just want to offer myself up and be his little lump of clay."

"*Marble*," Will corrected quietly.

"Excuse me?" Her blonde curls bobbed with the whip of her head.

"Michelangelo mostly worked in marble or bronze, with, I think, the *Two Spanish Fighters* being a one-off clay exception."

"My my, you are full of surprises, aren't you, Mr. Jessup?" She looked him up and down like an equestrian for purchase. "I had no idea you were so… *cultured.*"

You don't know a damned thing about me other than how my ass looks in boxer briefs, Will thought.

Will ran a hand through his hair. "You look incredible, Mrs. Kronin. Mr. Kronin has to be one happy man."

"*Pfft,*" Denise scoffed, waltzing through the grand foyer toward the rest of the house. Her heel clicks reverberated off of the lofty cream-colored walls and arched ceiling. "The ol' buzzard hasn't gotten back from Okinawa yet. Even then, I'm not so sure he'll even notice unless I order a custom neon sign to point to my chest."

Will followed close behind as she turned down a nearby hall and headed for the kitchen.

"I hate waiting around for him to notice me. I'm fairly certain he's having an affair. I don't like the look of his assistant. She's too… *perky.* They've been shacked up at the same Hilton the last two weeks for this tech deal he's been working on. It doesn't take a genius…"

She trailed off, making her way to the large dining room.

Will felt like he needed to say something to fill the silence. "If he cheats on you, Denise, the man is certifiably insane."

She laughed, high and haughty, and pressed her hands down onto the expensive, marbled slab of wood. "He married *me*. That alone *proves* the man is crazier than a shit-house rat."

"Hey," Will piped up. "You're a beautiful woman with a generous soul. I don't wanna hear you talking about yourself like that again, okay?"

"Sir, yes, sir!" She barked with a wink, putting up three manicured, ring-covered fingers to her upper forehead in her attempt at a military salute.

Will smiled at the bastardized attempt. "So, what's on the agenda today?"

"Well," she pointed behind her with a bony thumb, "today will just be the den, two of the guest rooms, and the upstairs bathrooms, mostly. Oh, and I have a few ladies coming over to, sort of, assess the services you offer. You know, to see if you'd be a good fit for them. More work-widows like myself, but ones with *old money*." She leaned across the table, drinking in the sight of muscles bulging ever-so-slightly out of Will's army costume. "One of them is *cousin* to a *second* cousin of a *Rockefeller*." She whispered the last word like a dirty secret.

"Oh," Will said flatly.

"They've been curious if you're any good. I told them you're fabulous, but they insist on seeing for themselves. I'll pay an additional fee, of course."

"I wasn't going to ask—"

"No bother. I *insist*. More eyes, more money. Like in a gentleman's club." Denise snickered as if what she'd said was some kind of joke. "Most of these women just want to watch a *man* clean for once, and this beats the hell out of the bloody Mary brunch at the club." Her eyes popped open wide. "Oh, that reminds me. Julio?!"

Will swallowed hard, looking around at the spotless dining room. There was almost never anything for him to truly clean in these expensive homes.

Denise shouted over her shoulder loudly. "Goddammit, *Julio*!"

A moment later, a small, middle-aged Latino man scuttled in with a potato in one hand and an old-school peeler in the other. His apron was crisp and freshly starched.

"Yes, ma'am?"

Will detected the slightest hint of a Cuban accent despite the man trying his best to hide it.

"Julio, fetch me a bloody Mary, would you, darling?" Denise never made eye contact with her servant, asking the question over her angora-covered shoulder pad.

"Yes, ma'am." Julio bowed slightly and turned back toward the kitchen.

"Oh, and Julio?"

"Yes, ma'am?"

"Make it extra spicy." She smiled at Will, back still turned to her chef.

"Of course, ma'am."

"And put in those pickled green beans I like."

But Julio was already gone. Will fidgeted with his fake dog tags.

"Come, Will. Get your supplies. You can start turning down the guest rooms upstairs, and then once the ladies arrive, you can do the baseboards and scrub the grout around the guest baths. You know, something down low to really show off your… *assets*." Stubborn wrinkles formed at the edges of her mischievous eyes.

Will forced a smile and a polite nod. "Will do."

"My husband's sister is coming into town next week and bringing all the kids, so I want it to look immaculate."

"Understood." Will nodded. "I'll hop to it, then." He pointed toward the kitchen, and she nodded. He waltzed in. White cabinets and state-of-the-art appliances glimmered. He smiled at Julio and grabbed some cleaning supplies from the pantry, as usual.

"Oh, and Will, dust the fan blades upstairs, too, would you?"

"No problem. Happy to be of service."

Julio handed the bloody Mary over to Denise, and she snatched it greedily, swirling the stick of celery to clink the ice cubes. The chef held up the jar he was tightening. "I put extra pickled green beans in there for you."

Denise moaned after downing a mouthful of the beverage. "Outstanding."

Julio nodded and walked over to put the jar away in the refrigerator near Will. He eyed the man's costume. "Military man today, huh? Nice. Army fatigues. Oh boy, those bring me back."

"Were *you*... in the military?" Denise asked.

"Yes, ma'am, I was," Julio murmured. "Army. During Desert Storm, ma'am. That uniform brings back some memories."

"Thank you for your service," Will uttered reverently.

"What about you?"

"Oh," Will felt his face redden with slight embarrassment, "I... uh... it's just a costume." He pointed to his "Sgt. Sexy" name tag.

Julio chuckled. "Ever heard of stolen valor?"

"Yes, sir, I have. I—"

"I was just giving you the business." Julio shook his head, laughed, and returned to peeling potatoes for the dinner he was preparing.

"I'll meet you upstairs in a few. I'm going to change. In the meantime, *get that cute little butt of yours to work!*" Denise shouted like a drill sergeant, holding three fingers to her Botox-deadened forehead again.

Will and Julio both snickered at the sight.

"Mrs. Kronin, remind me later to teach you a proper salute." Julio shook his head.

6

"I'm stiff as a board every morning when I wake up," the elderly receptionist croaked, readjusting her cat-eye glasses. "Without my yoga, I can't limber up enough to leave the gosh-darned house. Thank *God* my granddaughter suggested it to me when I was doing physical therapy for my hip. It's been a life changer. You remind me a lot of her, actually."

Ava listened intently, perched on the black leather chair beside the open office door. "I'm glad you can find anything to give you relief, Marge. I remember when you left us over there at Burton. There was this huge void that couldn't be filled."

"Oh, Ava, the stress over there was too much for me to handle, and that guy, Gary, was driving me insane. So uptight and type-A. Stress and chronic pain are a recipe for misery. I had to do what was best for me."

"Arthritis sounds horrible."

"Oh, you learn to live with it. You'd be amazed what your body can learn to tolerate over time, unfortunately." Marge pushed herself back from her walnut desk and pivoted her swivel chair towards Ava. "It's all about the mindset. The brain is a resilient thing. Where the mind goes, the spirit follows."

"I love that you have found a way to cope with the pain. Do you think the mind leads the spirit, though? Or do you think it follows your heart?"

"Following your heart is overrated, dear."

Ava's eyes glistened beneath the warm halogen light as she recoiled, shocked. "What?! Marge! I always pegged you for the hopeless romantic type."

"Romance… is… *fleeting*," Marge began, enunciating words with wrinkled lips and teeth stained from a lifelong affair with dark-roast coffee. "The heart is a curious, wandering thing whose needs and desires are ever-changing. It's hard to embrace the bad with the good and not try to change it, all the while keeping logic at the center of everything. Some days, it's hard. *Real* hard."

"How long have you been married, Marge?"

"Let's see… Janet and I have been together for… thirty-six years but married for eight."

"Wow. Incredible." Ava smiled. Her eyes flitted to the ornate painting she'd given Marjorie for her birthday last year. It now sat in a distressed wood frame just above the woman's otherwise bland desk. "Got any advice for me in that arena?"

Marge tapped a long, bubblegum-pink nail against her matching lipstick. A thought popped into her head. "Yeah, I do. In this life, you're gonna make mistakes, but if you're gonna look like an idiot for *any* cause… let it be *love*."

"Well, I've already looked stupid for it before. You know, with Dan."

"Oh, hush, child. I've known you how long? Stupid is the last thing I'd ever use to describe you." Marge folded her arms across the chest of her cable-knit sweater. "Life's never done making us look like fools, Ava. But love is the one thing worth going out on a limb for."

Ava couldn't hide the optimistic grin that spread across her face.

"Ava?" A woman's voice wafted out from one of the open office doors.

Marge flashed her a toothy smile and pointed to one of the rooms. "Ms. Rivers will see you now." She fluttered her fingers in a wave as Ava made her way into the office.

"Go ahead and close the door behind you, hun," ordered a middle-aged woman with a skunk stripe of white amid her black head of hair.

"Hello, Ava." The woman motioned to the chair on the other side of the L-shaped office desk. "Take a seat. It's a pleasure to meet you."

"Thank you for the opportunity," Ava said brightly as she sat.

"No problem. I'm Jessica Rivers. I take it we're interviewing you for one of our accounting positions here at the Jarvis Management Group, correct?"

"Yes, it's a pleasure to meet you, Ms. Rivers," Ava said, extending her hand to shake.

Not too hard, like a gorilla. Not limp like a noodle. But firm, with eye contact. All of her business management courses flooded back to her in an instant.

"I *love* your suit, by the way," Jessica added, motioning to Ava's attire.

Ava glanced down at her burgundy blazer and skirt. A delicate, lace-trimmed camisole peeked out from beneath the edge. "Oh! Thank you."

Jessica skimmed her eyes over the paper resume in front of her, making swishing noises with her mouth as she read. "It says here you worked as the Chief Revenue Officer of Burton Laboratories?"

"That's correct."

Jessica glanced up from the resume with raised brows. "You are aware this is an *accounting* position."

"Yes, I am. And I look forward to returning to a position that is closer to what I got my degree in."

"I see here that you have a Masters in Business Management from Jacksonville University."

"Yes, that's correct."

Jessica looked up with only her eyes, scrutinizing Ava's face. "Why go all the way to Jacksonville for that degree?"

"I was young. I wanted to get out on my own and see what life was like elsewhere. In the end, it made me really appreciate Wyoming. Florida wasn't for me. In fact, I really didn't care for it at all, but I stayed until I completed the degree. I finish what I start."

"You're committed."

Ava nodded. "I bloom where I'm planted."

"Well…" the woman's eyes shifted over the resume again, "Frankly, Ava, I hate to say it, but I think you're a little overqualified for this position."

Dammit! I knew this was coming, Ava thought.

"With all due respect, Ms. Rivers, I've been lucky enough to have experiences beyond my degree in the twelve years I worked at Burton Labs, but I'm eager to get back to my roots, and I am certain I could do that here at Jarvis. I've studied your business before the interview, and I'd be an asset to your team. You've had quite a growth spurt in the last few years. Jarvis is very philanthropic with what seems to be a mandatory community service agreement. You're a business that puts emphasis on its image, and I'm here to contribute to that with my previous experience as a financial advisor."

Jessica gave a tight smile and nodded. "According to your previously assumed responsibilities, it seems like you were involved in both acquisitions and corporate finance. That's quite a juggling act."

"I've never shied away from a challenge. Digging into the heart of a company, seeing how it operates, seeing where its strengths and weaknesses are… I feel like I bring a lot of experience and valuable insight with me here."

Ava watched Jessica's eyebrows climb up her forehead, worried that it would eventually become a part of her hairline.

"That might be the case, but let's say I hire you. You work here for a few months, and then a better position comes along, and you jump ship. See why I can't risk hiring someone with your advanced career history for an almost entry-level accounting position?"

"Well, you can choose to look at it like that, or you can look at the possibilities of my potential upward mobility at what lies ahead here on the pathway to advancement."

Jessica laughed. "This is a family-owned company. The boss *and his son* work here. If you are looking for another gig as a CRO, like you were, or CFO, that is a *very* unlikely possibility."

Ava's heart sank. "Is there *any* upward mobility in the future?"

Leaning back in her squeaky office chair, Jessica interlaced her fingers. "We want someone that wants to work until retirement. Someone that we can count on to *stay put*. We can't afford to have people jockeying for a better position, especially when they have access to so much critical information. If you're in accounting here, you'd likely *stay* in accounting. There is a low ceiling that comes with that role."

Ava contemplated what having a ceiling at all would feel like.

Suddenly, she felt suffocated.

"I still think this could be a great fit," Ava lied. She smiled warmly. "I could be a valuable—"

A loud sigh escaped Jessica's red, matte lips, cutting Ava off mid-sentence. "Thank you for your time."

Ava felt her courage evaporate in a flash.

"Marjorie really seemed to like you. I was listening to the two of you out there. She has impeccable taste in character." Jessica's deceptively peppy tone contradicted the sinking feeling in Ava's gut.

"She and I worked together for years. She's amazing. You've got yourself a good one." Ava forced a sad smile and rose from the seat. "Good luck with filling the position."

"Thank you, Ms. Quinn."

With her chin raised, she left the room quietly, nodded to Marge in the reception area, and shut the front door behind her.

7

The frigid temperature seemed to slice right through the windows and vents, forcing the Denali's heater to fire full-blast. The overcast sky threatened to open up at any moment, promising to unleash inches of snow over the picturesque town. Pulling into the turnoff for Morad Park, all she saw was a sea of snow piled at least a foot high, obscuring the painted lines on the asphalt.

Ava pulled into a vacant corner and placed the vehicle in park. Just beyond the nearby treeline, she spotted Will bundled in a black down coat, dark beanie, and tight jeans, ones that seemed to effortlessly showcase the muscular ass beneath. His handsome face was alight, breath fogging the air around him as he excitedly tossed a tennis ball around for his spirited pug. The dog scrambled wild after it in a flurry of flung snow, diving frantically through the drifts like a chubby, fur-covered dolphin.

In the back seat, Kuda whined a melancholic song into the snot-smeared window, vocalizing his excitement. Unsure of what he wanted to play with more, his body trembled, eyes ping-ponging between the round, chartreuse object and the squat, wrinkled canine darting after it. His huge eyes and pinned-back ears made Ava snicker as she grabbed his leash and held on for dear life as he rocketed from the SUV. The force whipped her like a carnival ride, and she swung the door shut just as Kuda yanked her away with a fierce desire to join the other pup.

"Woah! Kuda!" Ava's hair swayed beneath the rim of a scarlet knit hat, one that matched the bold shade of her petticoat. Kuda tugged forward, jerking Ava's petite figure around with ease. She skidded behind, thick winter boots slick from the frozen mix of muddy snow.

Will's attention shifted to her. Stubble speckled the skin below his rosy cheeks and nose, eyes wrinkled in the corners from the smile Ava's arrival bright to his face. She was stunning, even bundled up.

Kuda finally stopped at the gate.

Ava found her footing and tugged to reign him in. "You go at my pace, buddy. Remember?"

Kuda pranced from one foot to the other with an almost electric rush of excitement. As Ava opened the gate, Kuda lurched again, tugging the leash right out of her gloved hand, nearly throwing her into a muddy snowdrift.

"Whoa! Kuda, no! Stop!" Ava shouted, frantic. The small raven-black pit bull sprinted away, dragging his leash in the slush.

Will's face was suddenly tense, unsure if the sixty-pound canine would attack his seventeen-pound pug.

The dogs quietly wound like a yin-yang, sniffing nearly every inch of the other. Kuda investigated the pug's pink fleece sweater and abruptly crouched down on his front paws, lowering himself to eye level with the pug. His butt wiggled as he playfully barked at Gremlin.

Skidding on a patch of black ice on the walking path, Ava caught herself on something hard in the air just before she fell.

"Easy there. You okay?" Will asked.

"Yeah," Ava sucked in a deep lungful of ice-cold air, shocked at the near-fall and the actions of her unruly dog.

It was only *then* that she looked down and realized what she'd latched onto during the fall…

Will's arm was outstretched, flexed hard in her grasp, hard as a two-by-four. She stood straight and let his arm go slowly, trying to hide her shock at how strong and unwavering his arm was.

"Thank you. That could have been bad." She felt her cheeks grow beet-red, hoping he would attribute it to the frigid air.

Will snatched up his pug by the armpits and held the fat little thing up for Ava. "*Say hello to my little frien'*," he mocked in his best Pacino voice. "This is Gremlin."

The dog looked like it was tiptoeing in the air like a ballet dancer, and Ava laughed, petting the thing softly on the head. "Nice to meet you, Gremlin." She looked back at Will. "I suppose you can't get her wet or feed her after midnight?"

Will chuckled and put the dog down in the snow. "Something like that."

Gremlin bee-lined for the Pit Bull once released. She reared back, raised a paw, and bopped Kuda on the snout. In that instant, it was like a snare trap had been sprung. They were off, frolicking with carefree abandon through the snowy path up ahead. Kuda sprinted up the slick, shoveled walking path after Gremlin.

Then, as if a switch had been flipped, Gremlin was on the offense, chasing the Pit Bull in huge, circular laps through the snowy field near the river like the rippled rings of a rock thrown into water.

Ava and Will snickered, watching the two dogs play as though they'd always been long-lost friends.

"Wow." Will laughed. "Your boy's got a lot of energy. Gremlin's gonna sleep *so* good later."

Suddenly, the furry duo stopped cold, looking into each other's eyes, bodies board-stiff. Kuda took off running. Gremlin trailed behind, huffing and wheezing as she tried to keep up.

"It's nice to see Kuda have a friend. Not a lot of people trust pit bulls."

"Never met a mean one." Will smiled.

"Same. They're misunderstood."

"Don't get me wrong. Piss off a pitty, and they'll do some damage. But, then again, so will just about any dog."

Ava laughed as the racing canine missiles made another flurried lap around them.

"Thanks for comin' out."

"Thank you for the invite." Ava could feel herself blush again as she stood beside Will, staring out at the slow-roiling water beyond the dog's play area. "I've been meaning to check this place out for a while. Kuda seems to love it here."

"Yeah, Gremlin gets so excited whenever she goes for a car ride. She always knows we're comin' here."

"I'm definitely going to have to bring Kuda more often."

"So…" Will tucked his chilled bare hands into his back pockets, "besides bein' dragged around by him, what do you usually do for fun?"

"Fun… hmmm, fun… I feel like I know that word from somewhere," she joked, tapping a gloved finger against her chin to think.

Will snickered.

"I read. And I paint."

"You *paint*?" Will seemed genuinely impressed.

"Don't get excited. I mostly just do those silly little paint-by-numbers. I enjoy letting my mind sort of go on autopilot and then having something beautiful to show for it."

"Those paint-by-numbers still take skill. Ever tried painting anything original?"

"Yeah, I have. Twice. I audited a class at the community college, and they were always having us paint weird things. I remember doing one of a fruit bowl with bananas and grapes and stuff. The other was a spray bottle with a pair of those yellow dish gloves underneath. Both were atrocious. They both looked like a four-year-old's handiwork, but I still really enjoyed it."

"Aw, I'm sure they looked great. You still have either of 'em?"

"Last year, I hit a busted tire on the highway, and the SUV had a small leak. Think I used the fruit bowl to protect the garage floor from oil 'til my mechanic could get me in."

Will chuckled at the mental image of that. "What about all the paint-by-numbers? I don't remember seeing any in your house."

For a moment, Ava had forgotten Will had already been inside her house. She still knew so little about him.

"I don't hang them up. It's just a little something I do for fun. There's a little plaza over there on Maple Street where I usually donate the nicer ones when I'm done."

"Oh no kidding, my daughter's pediatrician's on Maple." There was a silence between them for a moment, filled with nothing but the gentle whoosh of the icy breeze, the jingle of identification tags, and the heavy panting of two excited dogs. "Wait a sec, did you do one of a girl with her arm around like a red fox?"

Ava could only smile and bashfully bury her pink face beneath the collar of her petticoat.

"That's *you*? You did that?" Will seemed shocked.

Ava nodded slightly, eyes unable to hold his intense gaze. Slowly, like a turtle, her face emerged again. "What about you? What do you do for fun?"

"Well, due to my, um, *unique* job, I have to stay fit, so I go to the gym quite a bit."

"Ew, for fun?"

Will laughed and shook his head. "I spend a lot of time teaching my daughter about classic cinema."

Kuda and Gremlin erupted in a symphony of barks for a moment before taking off again, romping and tumbling playfully into each other in the snow.

"I'm also a pretty avid reader," Will continued.

"Oooh, color me impressed. I don't see that often."

"What? Maids who can read?"

"No, just… *men* reading. I guess that's a tad sexist." She glanced up at him and then shifted her eyes down to the snow at her feet, nudging some of the slush into a neat pile with her boot. "What genres do you read?"

"I'm a sucker for romance." He smiled bashfully.

"*Seriously*?"

His tone grew quiet as if he was passing along a secret in a room full of people. "Seriously, there's like… a *lot* of steamy stuff in some of those." His eyes bulged.

"One of womankind's best-kept secrets, I suppose."

"I also love a good legal or political thriller. Or even a good, binge-able mystery series."

"A little murder and intrigue with your mysterious sweetness?"

"Yeah," he kicked at a small, yellowed snowdrift, too, "somethin' like that. I have a whole bookcase full of Grisham and Patterson at home. Bingeing my way through Castillo's *Burkholder* series right now. It's so good."

"I'm still stuck on what you led with." She giggled. "I gotta say, most men wouldn't admit that they read romance."

"True. I think some men view them as some sort of competition. I think guys think they can't live up to the men in the books, and that can be threatening. But the way I look at it, it's more like a guide to what women want, what secretly drives them wild. It's also good for me, professionally, sort of like research. When they hire me, women don't want some single-dad divorcee who is just trying to pay his bills. They want the male fantasy. Most want to feel desire. They want to feel heard. They want to feel powerful."

"Oh, I see. So reading those is like having a sexy secret weapon of sorts." Ava smirked and found herself hopelessly lost in his shockingly blue eyes. His features were lit up, and his smiling face made her soften.

He was a man. A real man. Open and passionate. And that physique… even in the dead of winter, she felt herself warm at the thought of it. The way the lines of his clothes hugged his body…

"*Right*." His voice snapped her from her thoughts of what he looked like wearing the snug policeman's uniform on her front porch. "I also really enjoy the concept of two people going down these totally different paths having to overcome all the odds and fight for their happy-ever-after."

Ava felt stunned as he spoke, nodding in agreement.

"Life is full of ups and downs," he continued, "and, sure, a lot of the time things don't work out. But with a good book, you get to feel that rush of euphoria over and over again. It's like a drug."

Gremlin deviated from her wide, circular path and darted toward her owner, hurtling her grunting body between his feet at top speed. Kuda followed the exact same trajectory, bowling Will backward with the force of the dog's strong impact against his thighs.

"Oh, f—"

Will landed on his back with a hard *thwap* in a patch of brown, muddied slush.

At least, he *hoped* it was mud.

"Oh no! Kuda!" Ava squeaked, kneeling beside him in the slurry. "Oh my God, are you alright? I'm so sorry, Will!"

As Ava spoke, suddenly, the pain from his fall felt dulled. Instead of feeling the sting of concrete against his hip, tailbone, and shoulder, he felt warmed by her touch, soothed by the sight of her. He glimpsed the porcelain face beneath her curtain of long hair, colorful and vibrant against the bleak, gray sky. She was a vision of red waves, her locks in sharp contrast to those jungle-green eyes. He felt like he could look at her for *hours*, studying every curve of her inviting mouth, flawless skin, and fluttering eyelashes with the appreciative gaze of an artist staring at an exquisite creation.

Was it the hard fall that stole the air from his lungs? Or was it that she had the single most *arresting* gaze he'd ever seen?

His heart thrummed hard in his chest. It had been so long since he'd felt every fiber of his being surge with excitement, and even then, it had never felt quite like *this*.

He saw her perfect lips moving but remained too focused on the gloved hand cupping his cheek to hear a word she'd said.

"Huh?" he finally mumbled, catching his breath.

The coldness of the world flooded back, along with the sound of her voice finally carving its way through the fog in his mind.

"I said, 'Are you alright? That was a hard fall.'"

"Oh. Mmm-hmm," he answered, dazed. His eyes glanced at her lips, and he wondered how they tasted.

"Here, let's get you up." Ava rose to her feet and held out her hands to help him.

Cold slush seeped through the back of his jeans, soaking the bare ass beneath them with a blast of frigid liquid.

As Ava helped Will to his feet, the sound of panting wafted toward them. They both turned their heads in shock.

Kuda was humping Gremlin.

They shouted the dog's names in unison, but the animals kept at it, pounding away like long-time lovers after a lengthy absence.

Nothing short of a fire hose was going to break them apart.

Ava covered her mouth with her hand, trying to stifle her laughter. "He's neutered, I promise."

"She's spayed," Will offered, tilting his head in curiosity at the scene."

"What do... we do?" Ava's giggles grew louder. She turned her back to the dog and shielded her periphery with her flattened hand.

"I guess if they're both... *you know,* maybe... we let them have their fun."

Something about the sudden flush of her cheeks and the sound of her genuine laughter made it nearly impossible for Will not to run his fingers through her hair, grip the nape of her neck, and pull her lips to his.

Slow it way down, Will.

This time... it's different. I can feel it.

Will turned his back to Ava to glance at the dogs again and then whipped his head back around with a grimace.

"Uh," Ava made a face, "you have... um..."

Will sighed and looked up at the stormy sky. More snow was in the forecast. "Do I have... dog shit on my back?"

Ava bit her lip and nodded.

"*Awesome.*" Will shook his head.

Ava tried not to laugh. "I got to admit. I was a little intimidated driving over here today. This has... sort of helped."

"Intimidated of what?"

"Of you." She blushed and looked down at the murky snow around her boots.

"Why would you be intimidated by me?"

"You're… *you know*." She gestured up and down his body with her gloved hands. A mischievous grin spread across his face.

"No. I don't." He laughed.

"Come on. In your line of work? Don't pretend like you don't know you're handsome as hell."

Will looked away, trying to hide the grin on his face from the compliment. "Gremlin, come on, girl!"

Gremlin wandered to his side, panting hard, tongue hanging so far down it was nearly touching snow. Kuda trotted over to Ava, slow and playful.

"Kuda, I don't believe you! *Snap out of it!*" She swatted the air.

Will doubled over with laughter. "Did you just pull a Cher and quote *Moonstruck* to your pit bull? I'm… *impressed*, frankly."

Ava giggled, embarrassed, and turned her back to the humping dogs. "I am *mortified*."

"Eh, dogs have short lives. Too short. If they're both fixed. It's good to let 'em live a little, I think."

"I just don't know why he was humping her. He's got no…" Her eyes grew wide, and she threw her hands up in an over-the-top shrug.

Will clipped Gremlin's leash onto her collar. "Well, I have to go and change and take like a million showers now. But we should do this again sometime."

"Not *this*, per se." He motioned to the dogs. "But, you know, like… *us*."

"Yes, let's." Ava pulled a set of keys from her coat pocket and picked up the leash Kuda had been dragging through the snow the entire time.

Ava held the gate open for him and Gremlin.

"And give you the perfect view of my feces and mud-soaked backside, no thank you. Ladies first."

He motioned to the gate, and she fought another snicker at the ludicrous mental image before leaving with her dog in tow.

Will followed close behind. "hey, you ever been to *The Million Dollar Cowboy*?"

"No. I know of it, but I've never been." Ava smiled, feeling herself blush at what she would assumed would come next.

"How about we go grab a drink? Say Wednesday? Seven o'clock?"

Ava fought the urge to squeal with joy, instead pretending to be calm. "Yeah, that sounds great."

"It's a date, then."

He stripped off his jacket, folded it poo-side in, and tossed it on the passenger-side floorboard.

Gremlin hopped in, dusting the upholstery in snowy paw prints.

Will climbed in the driver's seat and waved. She returned the gesture, beaming, and drove slowly out of the slick parking lot entrance back onto the main road. Will sat for a moment staring at the steering wheel, butt chilled, hip aching from the rude landing. He thought about the moment she touched him, on his back in the snow, when his body tingled with the electric current of something special.

She had only been gone from his life for thirty seconds, and he already wanted to be around her. He couldn't wait to see her again. The need was strong.

…Almost as strong as the desire to burn his disheveled coat. Mud, watery runoff, unknown dog crap, and wet pug. He would never fully get the smell of today out of it.

8

As she walked across the crowded street, Ava wondered why she agreed to the date and why, *on God's green earth*, she let Madison, of all people, *dress* her.

Not having gone on a date with someone other than Dan in nearly eleven years, she was beyond rusty. The dating scene seemed foreign to her. There were apps for everything now with swiping involved, painful amounts of topical chit-chat, and loads of lingo she was sure she'd never get the hang of. Like 'hooking up'? Was that *kissing*? Was it *banging*? She was always too embarrassed to ask when Madison used the term.

Should she mention her divorce?

Was this just going to be a fling?

Of all of the eligible women in Jackson Hole, most of them wealthy beyond measure, how was *she* the one heading to a date with Will Jessup? He was a man with an ass that looked like it had been sculpted out of marble and a jawline sharp enough to cut a steak with. How was he possibly single and interested if he's not a psycho?

Oh my God, is he a psycho?

She passed by the front window of *The Million Dollar Cowboy Bar* and stared up at the bulb lights curving along the fun font of the marquee. Above it, a large metal 'buckin' bronco' hovered. It was the infamous symbol plastered on damn-near everything around the state of Wyoming. Behind the signage stood a large, snow-dusted hill eclipsing the nearly-set sun.

The place was packed, as it often seemed to be, even for a weekday. Ava stood on the sidewalk, debating whether to turn and run or brave the popular hangout spot.

She slowly exhaled a gust of hot fog, straightened her posture, and waltzed inside with a faux confidence that would impress even the harshest acting coach.

The laughter, shifting glasses, twangy country music, and loud conversations instantly assaulted her with a barrage of noise. The smell of yeasty craft beer, cocktails, and sweat filled the air. Amplifiers from a live honky-tonk band carried vibrations through the wood up through the short carpeted runners. There were lively people everywhere, chatting, howling, and enjoying life. As Ava took her first few steps inside and removed her coat, her eyes enlarged as she took in the place as a whole, like some chaotic, country version of *Where's Waldo.*

Having stayed hidden away for the last few months, suddenly being plunged into a fishbowl of so many people felt suffocating.

Off-white walls were adorned with garnet inlays. The walls and corners were trimmed with dark wood, whittled into lumpy oak bears every so often. A room to the side housed several billiard tables with well-worn edges, pool sticks lining the walls.

In the main room, sandwiched in between two large glass display cases with taxidermied black bears and mountain goats, sat a long bar cramped with people. Worn saddles were mounted on pipes and bolted into the floor as clever stools, complete with stirrups. Various liquors and taps lined the mirrored back wall.

Aha, there you are, Waldo...

Ava finally spotted Will beside a saved seat, well-dressed in a powder blue button-down shirt and black slacks. She bit her lip. Something about a man in a button-down shirt made her instinctively want to rip it off. Will was no exception.

She stood for a moment, watching him sip his beer. Every move he made was suave. Controlled. *Intentional.*

The warm lights cast a bronze hue on him that would make a statue jealous. Everything on him was neatly in place and clean, from the flawless honey-blonde hair to the shine on his dress shoes.

His calm, easy manner was the total antithesis of how Ava felt inside: Messy. Out of control. *Aimless.*

Two attractive brunettes sitting on saddle seats at the bar gawked at him, whispering to one another and laughing flirtatiously. They looked like they were trying to get him to buy them a drink, even though it was abundantly clear they'd already knocked back quite a few.

As Ava made her way through the throng of people, a young blonde in skin-tight jeans and an American flag crop top showcasing her trim stomach strutted over to Will from one of the billiard tables. She leaned against the bar top beside him, pointed down to his jacket in the empty seat, and offered a sly smile.

The sight of it all evoked strong feelings of jealousy in Ava's gut.

She wanted to turn on her heels and walk out, but something about being all dolled up and already there glued her heels to the strip of burgundy carpet beneath her.

What the hell are you doing, Ava? Have you seen that body? He can have any woman he wants!

Despite still feeling the burning sting of all of the cheating, she had to remind herself that

Will Jessup was not her ex-husband. It wasn't right to assume that Dan's failure as a husband equated to Will not being a stand-up guy. Hurricane Ava had thoroughly ravaged her own life with resounding waves of emotional mass destruction. She'd found herself unemployed and divorced in the wake of the shit-storm of accidentally un-ended Zoom calls and botched job interviews. She wasn't about to let herself implode all of this, too. She wasn't ready to add another casualty to the list.

Ava stepped forward, feeling the intense desire to reclaim all that she had wanted from life.

Will said something, and the blonde's smile faded. A moment later, she slunk back to her gaggle of awaiting girlfriends.

Maybe… just maybe… he is *one of the good ones.*

A smirk spread across Ava's face just as Will's startlingly blue eyes settled on her across the crowd. He waved her over with a smile.

As Ava made her way across the room, Will muttered quietly into the ether, "Of all the gin joints in all the towns in all the world… she walks into mine."

Forging her way through the busy establishment, Ava finally made it to the bar, took the saved seat next to him, and exhaled deeply. She took off her crimson petticoat, exposing a little black dress beneath. The low-cut neckline showed off a tasteful amount of milky cleavage (*Thank you, Wonderbra!*) The hem of the skirt skimmed her knees. She could practically hear her mother's voice squawking in her ears: '*The shorter the skirt, the shorter the relationship!*'

"Wow, you look…. *phenomenal*." He whistled. "Thanks for coming."

"Of course." Ava fought her body's urge to blush at the compliment.

Will's eyes fluttered down the length of her body, drinking her in slowly before returning to her clover-green eyes. "*My my*. That dress… I am speechless."

"Thank you." Heat radiated through her cheeks. "Madison picked it."

His eyes glinted with mischief. "Remind me to send her a *thank you* card."

Warmth seeped into her belly at the compliment, and his grin sent her nerves into overdrive. "You look great, too. It's no beat cop costume, but it'll suffice."

"Thanks. I almost came dressed as a gladiator tonight, but I decided on this at the last minute."

She chuckled. "Yeah, I'm sure these fine people appreciate that."

"What?" He flexed his arms out into the air and quietly growled. *"Are you not entertained?"*

Ava fired back a line from the same movie, *"He enters* Million Dollar Cowboy *like a conquering hero. But what has he conquered?!"*

Will's eyebrows raised, and his jaw dropped. "I am impressed!"

"I told you I like to watch movies." Ava shrugged with a smirk and waved two fingers to politely catch the attention of the bartender swishing past. He didn't acknowledge her.

"Hope you don't mind. I ordered one while I was waiting. I'm usually obnoxiously early to stuff like this." Will held up his half-downed beer and took another sip.

"Not at all. I'd have done the same." She turned to him. "Order a drink that is, not be early. I always have to rush just to be right on time."

Another bartender whooshed past, on a mission to break a ten-spot at the other register. He paid Ava no mind.

"So tell me, if I might be so bold as to ask, what was it that you, uh, *did* for a living?" He leaned in, trying to make himself heard over the Luke Combs cover dribbling out of the amps.

The woodsy undertones of his cologne made something inside of her stir.

Easy girl...

"I was basically like a sales rep. I worked for a large laboratory that purchased smaller labs around the world. We turn… sorry, turned… them into specialized hubs, swapping their existing equipment and staff to streamline results. Half the time, I had a lot of meetings and presentations from home, but the other half consisted of procuring and acquiring some of the international labs. I was gone a lot. They had me flying to Japan, England, Ireland… all over the world."

"Oh wow, it seems like it would be interesting to get to see all those places."

"It was. Especially on other people's dimes. Now, who knows when I'll have enough to travel abroad again." She leaned forward on her elbows, lifting her butt off the saddle, hoping the copious cleavage would help catch a bartender's attention. "I'll figure it out," she said, leaning back. "Thankfully, I had been saving up for a bit. Maybe during this transition, I can try to remember what *fun* is… or write a book or something."

"Ooooh, what would you write?"

"I dunno. They say to write what you know." She chuckled, making quotation marks in the air. "*How to Get Fired* by Ava Quinn has a nice ring to it."

Will laughed and sucked back the last foamy sip of his IPA. "Eh, we've all been there. It's times like these when you appreciate the people who help break your fall."

Ava's smile washed away like a tide. "Yeah, this job was hell on my marriage and friendships. But Maddy stuck around, thank God. I've never been more grateful to have her. Especially after the divorce."

Shit, shit, shit, don't bring up the divorce! Leave your baggage on the carousel, Ava. Now is not the time...

She clammed up, afraid to say more.

"I've never been married, so I can't pretend to know what that's like."

"*What*?" Ava's eyebrows crawled up her forehead. "You've never been married?"

"Nope."

"Ever been engaged?"

"No."

"Serious relationship?"

Will hesitated before nodding. "Only one that was ever serious. High school sweetheart."

"Fizzled out?"

"She cheated." He cleared his throat and waved at another bartender.

"One sec, hun," she said, briefly making eye contact.

"Oof. Sorry to hear that." Ava, unfortunately, could relate. "So, just the one?"

"Yeah, no one else ever hung around more than a month or two. Just never met the right person. Didn't want to waste anyone's time. Just kept things casual for a while."

Ava nodded, taking it all in. She nervously tapped the cardboard coaster in front of her, wishing there was a beverage on it.

"Some movies make it look so easy, but relationships are so damn hard sometimes."

"Amen. If I had a drink, I'd cheers to that."

He held up his empty glass, and she pretended to clink it with a pantomimed one of her own.

Ava suddenly thought back to her wedding day, back to the hope and optimism she'd felt while staring into the eyes of the man who she truly thought would be by her side forever. Now, the memory was tarnished forever. A stain on her brain that no amount of alcohol or sappy movies could scrub out. She forced a slight smile. "We grow around the pain, though. That stuff never goes away, but our capacity to handle it grows."

"Damn. Well put." He smiled.

The bartender finally bounced over to them and sighed dramatically. "Ugh! Sorry about that. Some sort of conference just let out at the hotel over there, and we got slammed all of a sudden."

The young woman's tits were pushed up to her chin in a skin-baring tank top with a cowl neck that hung so low patrons could practically see her navel. When she leaned forward on the counter, she gave Will a first-class ticket to the show of her lacy lavender bra. Ava watched, fighting to keep her mouth closed at the shameless display.

If Will noticed, he didn't show it. His gaze remained on her face with the dedication and restraint of a eunuch.

"Another?" the bartender cooed to Will.

"Yes, thank you," he answered, sliding over his glass.

"Yeahhhh, buddy." She snatched it off the bartop and turned to Ava, visibly less peppy. "And what can I get you, ma'am?"

Fuck, did I just get ma'amed? *How old does she think I am? I'm too young to be a ma'am! I'm only thirty-three, for God's sake!*

Ava swallowed her agitation at the moniker. "Lemon drop martini, please."

Will looked at her and made a silly face as if to say, '*That was not what I was expecting.*'

"You guys wantin' anything food-wise," the waitress asked as if reciting the question was as natural as breathing.

"No, thank you. Just the drinks, for now," Will answered politely before returning his full attention back to Ava.

The waitress nodded and silently walked away.

"So, tell me a little more about yourself. Madison has *colorfully* described you as a 'workaholic, out of work.'"

Thanks, Madison.

Ava relaxed into her saddle seat and turned back to Will. "Unfortunately, she's not wrong. I'm a bit of a go-getter. Sort of a shark in the water. Always moving. Normally, I drive hard toward my goals, but now I'm trying to figure out what they *are* exactly. At the lab, I was a big 'people person.' Always super outgoing."

"So… maybe you can become, like, a tour guide or something where you can be around a lot of people."

"Yeah, or, like, a *madame*," she added, immediately regretting the word as soon as it slipped from her red lips. "Sorry. Here I am, talking about sex workers on a first date. I'm just… rusty." She nervously chuckled, and her mind spiraled.

Did I just say sex on the first date? Isn't it something we are supposed to pretend neither of us are thinking about? Shit. Way to go, Ava.

"Second," he corrected.

"Hmm?"

"Morad Park was our first. Although, after my falling into slush and dog poo, I can see why you'd want to forget all about it."

Ava laughed. "No, I just wasn't sure if that technically counted. Felt like more of a hangout."

Will only smiled and rubbed a finger nervously across a knot on the wooden bar.

Ava nudged him with a knee. "How are you feeling, by the way? That was a pretty hard fall."

"I feel great. A full bottle of ibuprofen and some intense physical therapy, and I was right as rain, like, two days later."

Ava laughed. She wasn't sure when it had started, but her leg was jiggling full speed.

Will placed his hand on her knee to stop it. The heat emanating from his hand burned through the fabric, seeping into her freshly shaven flesh. "You have nothing to be nervous about."

She stared down at his hand and felt her heart ram against her chest like a raging bull locked in a cage. "At least I know better than to talk about my divorce, right?" She rolled her eyes to chastise herself, mind screaming, *'Stop talking!'*

Will removed his hand and placed it back on the bar. "I couldn't help but notice the photo in your hall of you in your wedding dress with the groom ripped out of the picture.”

The riotous butterflies in her belly settled, and a deep ache arose. “I keep it as a reminder. That was the best day of my life… so far. My goal is to replace it with a better one. Until then, it serves as a reminder to get out and do something worthy of framing again.”

“I like that. Using something negative to make a positive change.”

The drinks arrived. The bartender set the beer down carefully. “One beer.” Then, yellow liquid sloshed over the edge of the sugar-rimmed martini glass garnished with a lemon slice as she slid Ava’s brashly across the bar. “And one lemon drop martini.”

Will looked at Ava as the woman shuffled off.

“Wow. She *really* seems to like you.”

Ava laughed, glancing into Will’s eyes. She couldn’t seem to tear herself away. Those crystal blue orbs radiated all the warmth and comfort of being home beneath a blanket with a good book. As a smile graced his lips, they felt inviting.

She flashed a cursory glance over her martini, which seemed surprisingly spit-free despite the bartender’s apparent disdain for her. She took a sip and pinched her eyes closed. "Mmmm. Oh my *God*, that's good."

Even though the woman seemed like a bit of a bitch, Ava had to admit she made one hell of a martini.

Will was still enamored by the sound of her pleasurable moan, feeling the crotch of his dress slacks shrink a little at the sound.

"I gotta ask." Ava laughed. "How much did Madison pay you to clean my house in a police uniform?"

"I can't say." He smirked. "You know, maid-client privilege and all."

"*Oh.* Of *course*," her red-brown hair bobbed through the air, "the infamous maid-client privilege. How silly of me."

Will felt captivated by her smile.

"You seem like a smart guy, Will. You could probably do a million other things. So, why *this* profession?"

His smile faded, and his tone grew deeper. "My daughter, Starla, is a Type 1 diabetic. Her insulin is expensive as hell. I was a diesel mechanic making good money when she was diagnosed, and it was fine. But about a year and a half ago, the company laid myself and about eighty other people off. I couldn't afford COBRA. It was outrageous." Anxious, he picked at the design on the side of his glass with a short fingernail. "I couldn't afford her pump and her medicine otherwise. I had to improvise. I had to figure something out fast."

"Oh, wow. I'm so sorry."

He looked back up at her and gave a tight grin that didn't meet his eyes. "I was able to pay down the doctor's bills and get her medicine this way. And it's not a bad way to earn a living. I actually enjoy it a lot. I get to meet a lot of really interesting people. The work is easy. Hell, battling my pride was literally the hardest part of the whole thing."

"I think that's pretty admirable. You seem like a good dad. She needed something, and you did anything you could to provide it."

"I think I want to keep doing it, too. I've built up a nice little client base and filled out my costume collection." He smiled warmly at her. "I think soon I may even file for a business license."

"You got a name picked out for your company?"

"Nah. Maybe something short and simple like… *Jessup Cleaning*."

"That's… a name." Her eyes widened comically and then went back to normal. "Do you plan on staying a one-man operation? Or do you have goals to expand to, say, a fleet?" She took another sip of her martini and let out a tiny moan of satisfaction.

Will cleared his throat. The small little lip smacks, and the animated way she savored her drink was adorable. The way she licked sugar from her luscious bottom lip hypnotized him. He felt his dick twitch in his pants.

"I know a couple guys who might one day be interested, but I'm not sure if I want to grow like that just yet. I'm enjoying having it all to myself for now."

"How do you advertise?" she asked, genuinely intrigued.

"Word of mouth." He grinned. "Why? Thinkin' about hiring me again?"

She wagged a manicured finger at him. "No. And technically, I didn't hire you the first time. I ask because I have a bachelor's in business management with a minor in advertising. I was just curious."

"This is a date, not a *Shark Tank* pitch."

"You're right. You just piqued my interest. It makes sense. It's a low-overhead service in a niche market. Client's houses are going to keep getting dirty, so it's a recurring service with some predictable regularity if scheduling is done correctly. And I'm sure you're making a *mint* in tips by catering specifically to wealthy clientele who can not only afford to hire a maid but to hire one who cleans in accordance with their tailored fantasies." She shrugged and took another sip of her drink. "I commend you. It's a great idea."

"Thank you." Will leaned in a little closer. "I appreciate that. Thank you for not judging me or treating me like a stripper."

"There's nothing wrong with strippers. Sex work is real work. Plus, you're not just stripping. You're scrubbing and vacuuming and scouring, too."

"It's a dirty job, but someone's gotta do it."

"With the way you filled out that cop costume, I imagine it can be a *very* dirty job…"

Will leaned in, closer still. Ava could feel his body heat radiating through her clothes at such a close proximity. His voice was quiet and flirtatious, barely rising above the sounds of the nearby slide guitar. "*You have nooooo idea.*"

She rubbed her fingers absentmindedly along the stem of her glass. "How old is Starla?"

Will smiled brightly, face lighting up with momentary glee at the mention of his child's name. "She's six."

Ava plucked the lemon slice from the rim of her glass and stirred the dwindling remainder of her drink with it. "What happened to her mother? Is she… still in the picture?"

"About a year-and-a-half after Starla was born, my ex, Sarah, decided motherhood 'wasn't for her.' She wanted to party and stay out late, drinking all the time, while I wanted to be home with our daughter. We drifted apart, and eventually, she left. *Both* of us."

Ava's lips curled into a frown, and she rubbed the damp ring on her coaster. "I hate to see someone piss away the gift of being a mother like that. Fires me up. Some women don't know how good they have it. Some of us," she bristled, feeling the dam of emotions she could barely contain, "we don't ever get to be that lucky."

Her mind flashed to her fertility doctor, to the results of her viability testing, to the tear-filled weeks of wallowing in her own self-pity, to the nursery she later converted into an office after the official verdict.

Will placed a hand on hers and pressed his lips together with a sorrowful expression. He held it for a moment. She could feel the genuine compassion in the silent gesture.

"Another round?" the bartender cawed from halfway down the bar to Will.

"Yes, please," Will bellowed.

The bartender nodded, and Ava could have sworn the woman winked at him, too.

"Does Starla know why you have so many costumes?"

"She probably doesn't care much, to be honest. She's in her own little fantasy world unless I pull her out of it sometimes. She's a big reader."

"Oh yeah? What's she like to read?"

"She adores those little interactive choose your own adventure kinda books? Remember those?"

"I used to *love* those."

"They're making a bit of a comeback."

She smiled, remembering back to when she was a child, like a mouse in a maze, searching for the right ending. If only you could go back a chapter in her own life, like before she married Daniel, and do it over again to make the *right* choice.

"I am a classics lover myself," Will volunteered. "I recently just finished re-reading Journey to the Center of the Earth."

"Oh God, I haven't read that one since junior high."

"I love the classics. Movies, too."

"Pffft. You like classics?"

"Yeah."

"Like… black-and-white movies?"

"Yeah, of course."

"I *don't* believe you."

He chuckled. "Why?"

"You look like an action movie or sports drama kinda guy."

"What?!"

"You're buff as hell. You look like you have *Friday Night Lights* and *Rudy* memorized."

"Rudy's not bad, but it's no *Citizen Kane*, that's for damn sure."

"*You* like *Citizen Kane*?" Her tone was incredulous. She'd fully turned on her saddle stool to face him, body poised in disbelief against the bar.

"Yes. Why is that so unbelievable?"

"Because I love classics, too."

"No, you don't." He waved her away playfully. "You're a double-feature of *Legally Blonde* followed by *Miss Congeniality* kinda woman."

"I find that downright offensive," she joked. "If I'm watching a double-feature, it's going to be something like *Manhattan* followed by *The Last Picture Show*. Or back-to-back Ingmar Bergman flicks."

His eyes opened wide, stunned. "I don't want to be crass, but now you're just talking dirty to me."

She laughed.

"Oooh, baby. Say Ingmar Bergman again, but, like, real slow and sensual, like you just did."

The grin he flashed made her feel a rush of heat blast through her. "Alright, which is better? *The Seventh Seal* or *Smiles of a Summer Night*?"

"Trick question. The answer is *Wild Strawberries*."

Ava gasped and clutched her chest. "Wow."

"You alright over there?"

"Yeah." She looked stunned. "I *severely* misjudged you."

"Most people do. I'm more than just half a fireman outfit and a feather duster, you know." Will winked.

"I can see that now." Then, she pressed a fingertip to his knee gently. "Okay, now, big question…"

"Shoot."

"On the count of three, name your favorite black-and-white movie."

"Easy." He shrugged casually.

She counted off on her fingers in the air. "One… two… three."

"*Casablanca*," they both uttered in near-perfect unison.

Ava clasped both hands over her mouth to keep from gasping loudly.

Will's eyes bulged. The bartender set down their fresh round of drinks, and he chugged half of his beer in one go.

"No… effing… way," Ava finally whispered.

As Will's eyes returned to her, everyone else in the bar seemed to fade into obscurity.

They could feel an almost palpable magnetic pull forming between them.

Finally, Will muttered, "Louis, I think this is the beginning of a *beautiful* friendship."

Ava laughed.

Will stared at her for a moment, mesmerized. "You are absolutely stunning. I'm sure you get that a lot."

She shook her head, feeling her cheeks grow beet-red at the compliment.

Sensing he'd made her uncomfortable, he moved the conversation back to the prior topic. "That's crazy. We have the same favorite movie. I was just trying to show it to Starla the other day. I think she made it a whopping ten minutes in before she started snoring."

"Oh man, I love it. I just forced Madison to watch it with me the day before I saw you at the gym. That movie fills me with so many emotions. They don't make films like that anymore. Ones whose beauty transcends time. Never aging. Never going out of style."

"Those times had to be crazy to live in. No text messages or emails. No cheap fare discounts or travel Groupons. You fell in love hard and fast, and the best you could hope for were letters back and forth."

"Women were devoted. Men were sincere."

"No modern-day dating games—"

"...Just vulnerable, uninhibited passion." It was like she had finished his thought, both romanticizing monochromatic films as if they shared one mind.

"Those times had to be especially hard for women. The men got to be in charge. The women stayed barefoot and pregnant."

"No way, what about *Gone With the Wind*?"

She clenched her teeth and looked at him almost apologetically. "I actually haven't seen that one."

"What? And you call yourself a lover of classic cinema?! For shame, Ava."

"I know. I almost saw it once on seventy millimeter at an Alamo, but there was some sort of projection issue."

"Well, now I know what our next date'll be."

"Ooooh, very presumptuous. So there will be another date?"

"Won't there be?" Will asked, his expression was hopeful.

Ava shrugged and smiled, downing the last of her second martini. The cacophony of busting billiard balls, country crooners, riotous laughter, and loud conversations seemed to swell.

"It's loud. Would you maybe want to go for a walk?"

"Yeah." Ava nodded, looking around. "I can barely hear you in here."

Will fished out his debit card and held it out for the bartender. "Check, please."

The bartender nodded her blonde mop and scurried off with Will's card. Within a few moments, she handed him a pen and several receipts, one of which had a string of ten digits and the words 'call me, Carly' below. Will fought the urge to roll his eyes at the phone number as he scribbled his tip and signature.

Ava thanked him for the drinks, collected her things, tied the belt of her coat, and started for the exit.

"Wait." Will pulled open the front door of the bar, greeted by a wall of arresting air, and gestured to the frigid snowdrifts outside. "After you, beautiful."

***

"Which direction?"

"That way." Will pointed to the left.

Ava nodded in understanding and strutted out of the bar, sashaying the way Madison insisted, exaggerating the movement of her hips a little with every step.

Will studied her entrancing form as if she were a swaying pocket watch in the skilled hand of a hypnotist.

Nearly at the corner, Ava slipped in some half-frozen slush. Will lunged forward a step and steadied her. "Whoa. You alright?"

Ava nodded, clutching his arm closer to her ribs. Partly for stability. And partly because touching Will filled her with a giddy excitement she hadn't felt in…

Well, maybe *ever*.

They took a few more steps before Ava's worn boot tread slipped again. She tumbled, legs failing her like a newborn deer. Will thought fast and reached out, wrapping his arms around her, catching her before she could fall to the concrete. Suddenly stabilized, their bodies were pressed together. She could feel his abs pressing into her with every deep breath.

Ava looked up at him from inside his embrace, faces dangerously close. His irresistible smile broadened, making her knees feel like jelly.

"I've seen women fall for me before, but jeez," he said with a laugh.

The sound of it bulldozed Ava's defenses.

He gazed down, words catching in his throat. "I have a place in mind that I think you'd love. It's still a short trek, but it might be treacherous in those boots. Hold onto my hand for balance."

Ava nodded and interlaced her gloved fingers with his bare hand. She felt a sudden rush of heat race from her belly to her face.

As Ava waddled beside Will, she tried to remember the last time she'd held hands with anyone. It had to have been the better half of a decade, surely. Well before her wedding to Dan, before his chivalry disappeared for good, vanished like a feather in the wind. Before years of complacency and infidelity and nights spent pondering what she'd done wrong. Before the vicious fight about the positive pregnancy test laid in the kitchen trash…

A pregnancy test that wasn't *hers*.

A gust of wind dusted Ava's face with fine powdered snow, dousing her tainted trip into years past with a dusting of winter's icy glitter. She walked in silence, his hand bathing hers with a radiant warmth.

The man was a human furnace, she decided.

Will tugged gently and turned toward the door of one of the shops in the plaza.

Ava stepped back, pulling her hand from his to read the sign. "The *Mount Olympus Cafe*." Two faux pillars were stationed at each side of the door, lending the modest exterior a Greek theme.

"If you don't like coffee, this place makes a mean hot cocoa, too. They make their marshmallows in-house."

Ava moaned a little at the thought of it and smiled. Will held the door open for her, and they both wafted in with the cold. The scent of ground coffee beans and warm, frothed milk filled the air.

"I've walked past this place so many times but have never come inside."

"Well, tonight is a night of firsts," Will said, gently placing a hand against the middle of her back. "If they were open right now, I'd take you next door and buy you some *actual* snow boots. Like, ones with *tread*."

"Are you kidding me? These boots make my whole outfit," she joked.

"Oh. Of course. *Priorities*."

"Welcome to At the counter, a young woman with plum-colored hair in a messy bun greeted them. Her dermal piercings glinted in the dim overhead mood lights. Her eyes landed on Will and stayed there.

"Hello-welcome-to-the-Mount-Olypmus-Cafe," the woman said so fast that it all came out as one jumbled word. She sounded like she'd recently chugged a Big Gulp full of espresso.

Will blinked hard, unable to process how fast she'd spoken.

"What-can-I-get-for-you?" Again, her words all bled together.

"As good as that hot cocoa sounds, I need some *java*. I'll have, uh, a Helen of Troy," Ava said definitively, still staring up at the Greek-themed menu.

"The latte or frappe?" Finally, they were starting to turn into individual words. Still, the woman's gaze stayed fixed on Will.

"Latte, please."

The woman typed it onto the point-of-sale screen. "And you?"

Will smirked. "Surprise me. What's your favorite?"

The barista giggled. "Can't go wrong with the *Zeus Lightning Cappuccino*."

"I'll have one of those then, please." Will reached into his back pocket and whipped out his wallet.

"No, no. I've got this." Ava protested, laying her hand over Will's. "You got drinks at the bar. This is *my* treat." She unzipped the caramel-colored purse that perfectly matched her boots and rifled through the contents, looking for her wallet. Before she could produce any money, Will's debit card was eagerly taken by the barista.

"Will! I was going to get that. I believe in equality."

Will shrugged. "Old habits die hard. It's nice to spoil a good woman every once in a while."

The barista handed his card and receipt back with a bashful smile. Will was clueless about the cashier's dumbstruck display. "Thank you."

"I-I-it'snoproblem," she stammered, blending her words again.

Ava and Will wove their way through the tables, passing a few patrons. Some typed away on laptops or were enthralled in paperback novels. The clack of the keys, murmured phone calls, and scrape of ceramic mugs gave the cafe a quiet hum of life.

They took a seat beside a large front window with spidering frost that collected at the corners. A loud gust of wind whirled a layer of fine, white snow. The breathtaking view of the inky night sky hovered overhead, millions of stars visible. Will brought his focus back to Ava.

"So, have you lived in Wyoming long?"

"My whole life. Born and raised right there in Riverton, actually. Came to Jackson Hole when I moved back because of the airport."

"Came back? From where?"

"Jacksonville. Went there for a few years to get my Bachelor's."

"You had a taste of the beach life, and you came *back*?"

"Oh yeah. Florida's heat is absolutely brutal. And there wasn't much to look at if you're not dazzled by Spanish moss. Not like here." She motioned to the moon-kissed mountains outside. "I missed this Wyoming. To me, this is it. I've been all over the United States. Been to twelve other countries, too. I can honestly say I've never seen any place more captivating than right here. I know I'm not the only one, either. I always see tourists flood in, and new shops pop up every year. Turns out this place is not exactly a well-kept secret."

"Yeah, this state has grown a lot since I was a kid."

Looking into his sapphire eyes, she could feel her defenses weaken, walls cracking. Walls she had put in place for a reason. His gaze made the temperature of the room feel like it was rising to a rolling boil.

One side of his lip raised in a sexy grin that cranked her body temperature up to inferno.

"So what about you? You from here?"

"Casper, actually."

"Oh, nice. I've been there a bunch of times. What brought you to Jackson Hole?"

"The jackalopes," he said with a straight face.

Ava erupted into a sudden burst of loud laughter, one that turned the heads of nearly every person in the establishment. "Sorry," she said with the flourish of her hand to the others before covering her mouth with it. She tried hard not to crack a smile. "Jackalopes, huh?"

"Ohhh yeah," he said with mock seriousness. "They're good eatin'. Figured if I came here, as long as I could afford ammo, I'd never go hungry a day in my life."

Ava buried her face in her hands to keep from spooking the other patrons a second time with her laughter.

The infamous *jackalope* was the state's gimmick to earn tourists' money, stemming all the way back from the 1930s. Taxidermied bunnies with antelope horns glued to their heads remained a common staple at nearly every kitschy souvenir shop and antique dealer in the state.

"I'm obviously kidding." Will snickered.

"Oh, I assumed you were. Otherwise, this date was about to be over."

The barista wove her way through tables toward them with a cup in each hand. She set down Ava's brashly before placing one delicately in front of Will.

Avoiding Ava's glare, the barista gave Will a flirtatious smile. "If there's anything else you need, just let me know."

"Thanks." Will nodded.

Ava felt a pang of irritation as she watched the barista retreat. Women were hungry tonight. It seemed *Will* was on the menu.

Will held up his mug to cheers. "Here's lookin' at you, kid."

Ava forced a smile, still a little agitated at the barista, and clinked mugs with him. "Cheers."

"No, to answer your question…" Will's voice snapped Ava back into the moment. "I came here because it's beautiful, and I feel like there's room to breathe. I was going to CWC here when I found out we were going to be graced with Starla's presence. That obviously changed my path. I needed money, so I put my degree on hold. Kids are expensive."

"What were you going to school for?"

"Nursing. I wanted to be a traveling nurse. You know, see the world. Interact with people. I didn't want to be a doctor. I wanted to know the patients and actually *help*, you know?"

"Ever think you'll go back?"

"Doubtful, but who knows. I like what I do. It may not be as admirable, but I still feel like, with the cleaning, I'm helpful and serving people, making people's lives a little better. Now, Starla can have the stability she needs. She doesn't have to bounce around schools and stuff like she would've."

"Your daughter is very lucky."

"I don't know about lucky. It's been a challenge from time to time. She deserves the world, but at least I'm there when she needs me."

"That's more than a *lot* of little girls have."

"True. Thankfully, I feel like I'm getting a little better at this whole *single dad* thing."

"Oh yeah? How so?"

"Well, recently, I learned how to iron a pleated dress and do a half-decent ballerina bun."

Ava smiled at the mental image of Will ironing a dress. "Can I ask why things didn't work out between you and her mom?"

He sighed, knowing the question was coming. The sting still lingered in his chest. "We hadn't been dating long before Sarah got pregnant. Something like two months. Starla wasn't planned. Sarah and I *liked* each other a lot by then, but the *love* part never came. Years later, Sarah started hanging out with a weird crowd. She started doing a lot of things I didn't approve of. Acting less and less like a mother and more like a rebellious teenager. She still wanted to go out, see the world, and party as if she had no obligations. She'd disappear for, like, two days and come back with a hangover from Hell and offer no real explanation of where she'd been. Eventually, we had to have a come-to-Jesus moment, and I told her I didn't want to live like that anymore. I mean, last I saw her, she had tract marks all up her arm. I didn't want Starla to have to see that when she was older. So we split, and days later, Sarah went completely AWOL. A few months later, I ended up with full custody, and she ended up… who knows where. Haven't heard from her since Starla was about three when she came poking around wanting to see her." He eyed his drink. "Not everyone is cut out for parenthood."

"Wow, I'm sorry to hear that."

"Thanks." He sipped his drink and fidgeted with the cup's handle.

"That had to be such a rough time."

"It was. I'm not gonna lie. It really was. Right after my ex's little disappearing act, I found out Starla had diabetes, so getting her the right treatment was stressful. It was a lot to learn, even *with* the nursing courses I'd taken. It was a lot of trial and error."

"I'm sorry you went through that."

"Thank you." He shifted back against the leather of the booth with a squeak and watched the swirling steam rise from the lightning bolt drawn in the foam of his cappuccino. "So, since we are asking the hard-hitting questions, I know you have your fur-baby, Kuda, but do you ever want kids?"

Ava's heart sank. The words hit her like a cinder block to the stomach.

He should know now before we waste each other's time.

"It's sadly not in the cards for me. I unfortunately can't have kids," she said, voice laced with melancholy. "I really wanted them, but I've seen several specialists, and… it's just not the way my life was meant to go, I guess."

Will's eyes locked onto hers, apologetic and dazzling. "Oh my God, I am so sorry. I shouldn't have asked."

"No, it's fine. Better you know upfront. I know that's usually a deal-breaker for people."

Will shook his head and took a tiny sip of his piping-hot drink.

"I considered adoption or fostering, but my ex-husband, Dan, wasn't a big fan of either one. I didn't feel like it was fair for a child to only be truly wanted by one parent, especially when some come from such painful situations. So I threw myself into my work as soon as that door closed for me." She leaned back, mimicking his body language without thinking about it. "And, now, I don't even have that."

I have nothing to offer you. Hell, I have nothing to offer anyone right now, she thought.

A sting of embarrassment turned her cheeks pink. Her eyes told more of a sad story that her lips could never utter.

"I've made the most of it. I've seen and done all the things I wanted to do instead. I travel. I eat exotic foods. I've experienced different ways of life. And I'm sure I'd be a *lot* more stressed about losing my job right now if I had someone dependant upon me."

"Truth," Will said quietly with a nod. Their eyes locked for a moment. Ava felt suddenly giddy, her stomach clenched with excitement. Will looked away.

"So, what are your customers like?"

Will chuckled. "Well, none of them are quite like you, if that's what you're wondering. Most of them are excited to have a man cleaning their house in basically his underwear."

Ava blushed again and covered part of her face with her hand. "I'm sorry. Madison caught me off guard. It was bad timing. Plus, it's not every day I just let a total stranger rummage through my home, clothed or not."

"I get that." Will smirked. "The majority of my clients are awesome. I meet a lot of cool people doing what I do. Some of these people are new to being millionaires and tip obscene amounts of money for the basics. They're never gonna get on their hands and knees to scrub their own bathroom when they can afford to hire it out. But the costume thing just exploded with the lonely housewife crowd. They feel a little zing of naughty excitement using me for their cleaning… and *entertainment.* With their husbands being gone all the time, the wives are just looking for a cheap thrill. Plus, I genuinely enjoy cleaning."

"I wish I could say you caught me at a bad time, but that would probably be a bit of a fib. I can thrive in messy. *I* know where everything is."

"Yeah, not me. Since I was really young, I'd always help my mother around the house. She'd let me use the vacuum and showed me how to do the dusting. We'd listen to music, spray each other with water, and just enjoy time with each other. I loved that feeling you get from scrubbing out a stubborn stain and the accomplishment of looking at a clean room that was chaos before. People seem *lighter* when their home is in order. I'm helping people like I always wanted. Just… in a different way than I thought I would. Plus, the scheduling gives me the flexibility to be there like I *want* to be for my daughter. I want to pick her up from school and go to her recitals and choir performances. I want to be there to monitor her sugars, make sure she's eating right, and tuck her in at night."

"Do you have any family around to help with her?"

"Nope. My father are old-fashioned conservatives. I have barely talked to them since my daughter was born... *out of wedlock*. My parents had a huge problem with that. They retired just after she was born and moved down to Boca Raton. Barely heard from them since." He shrugged. "My brother and I aren't really close either. He moved down to Florida to be near them. So, it's just me."

"Wow, I didn't realize."

"Yeah, my neighbor's daughter babysits from time to time, like tonight, but it's mostly just me and Starla."

"I'm sorry your family's so distant, but they're the ones who are really missing out in the end."

"Yeah." Will sounded quiet, unsure.

"...And what is it with people and Florida? I didn't like it there. It's like everyone thinks it's some sort of mecca or something."

"It's certainly not for me. I like the snow. Feels like they have one season year-round down there."

Ava smiled. "I'm glad you're there for your daughter. There are a lot of deadbeat fathers in this world. It's nice to see one that cares as much as you do. And, not to toot your horn *too* much, but from a business perspective, if it's any consolation, I think your service is fairly genius."

"You can toot my horn anytime." Will smiled playfully. "Yeah, I can't believe how much it's already grown in such a short time. I started out with one client, and now I have so many that I've had to start a wait-list. I only showed up at your place because Madison called in a favor."

"Well, now I feel like an ass."

"Don't." He waved a hand at her. "But yeah, I enjoy what I do for the most part. And the money's great. Hell, I'll stand on my head or do a jig for what they pay me. I don't mind looking a little silly if it makes people happy. I get to do what I enjoy, and ultimately, I take a lot of pride in knowing I made people's lives a little bit better and made their day a little bit brighter."

"I've never met a man who enjoyed cleaning." Ava chuckled. "You certainly are a unicorn of sorts." She scoffed. "Hell, most of us are lucky to find one that can get their clothes *in* the hamper instead of on the floor *beside* it. Drives me insane."

Will smirked. "Yeah, it's way too commonplace." He stared out the frosted window for a moment and then returned his eyes to her. "I wouldn't say this is the best long-term gig. Eventually, I'll age, and scrubbing on my old knees will get old. People will start paying me to keep my clothes on."

Ava laughed at that.

"But for now, it works. It would be cool one day to manage like a fleet of other men doing the same thing. What would that make me? Like a pimp or something?"

"Not unless they're doing a lot more than cleaning." She giggled. "I'd say supervisor or manager would be more apt."

"Right." a handsome smile curled onto his lips. His eyes traced the delicate line of her neck to the feminine curves of her collarbone beneath the lapel of her petticoat. Her skin looked sensitive like it might respond to the brush of his stubble or a trail of soft downward kisses.

"If you wanted to expand, you could make exponentially more." She was starting to sound like a financial advisor, tugging Will from his momentary fantasy of where he wanted to press his lips…

"It seems like you have a good client base already established," she continued. "There's very little overhead beyond, what, gloves, gas, and costumes? You don't even have to buy your own chemicals so that even lessens your expenses—"

"Whoa." He held up a hand. "Are we on a date or a business meeting?"

"Sorry." She looked truly embarrassed, flashing her green eyes to freezing passersby out the window, brushing past arm-in-arm. "You're right. I apologize. I wasn't trying to overstep. I just know a good business idea when I see it. Seeking out businesses with wider potential was my sole job for over a decade. *Occupational hazard.* My apologies."

"So what is it that you want to do now? Can you do the same for another corporation?"

"No. I signed a hefty five-year non-compete. Standard for my field. By then, so much will have changed, and I'll be too far out of the loop, finger off the pulse of what's a good buy and what's a waste of time and effort. A totally new avenue is, unfortunately, in order. It's just overwhelming."

"I can only imagine. But you're bright. You're a no-nonsense woman who takes no shit, I can tell."

"Oh, I still have plenty of nonsense," she chuckled.

"Oh, *please.* What's your nonsense? You're a little messy? Got some baggage. Not a biggie. What else you got? A designer clothing addiction? An *Only Fans* foot fetish page?"

"Come on. Nobody would subscribe to see my *Only Fans,*" she grumbled.

"I mean, you'd have one subscriber right here." He bounced his thick, manicured brows.

His flirty words made Ava's stomach do somersaults.

Will finished off the last sip of his cappuccino.

She motioned to her own drink. "This is delicious. You were right about this place."

"You should try my coffee. Oof, I make a *mean* mug."

Ava nodded, trying to hide her smile. "I'd like that."

"What are you doing Friday evening?"

Ava's eyes bolted from her coffee to his in a flash. "Huh?" She wasn't certain she'd heard him right.

"Well," he looked at his watch, "I only have my babysitter for another twenty minutes, but Friday, Starla's spending the night at her friend's house. I could do some light fare or charcuterie or something and make you one of the best cups of java you've ever had in your life."

"Bold statement." She arched an eyebrow at him.

"I can back it up. What do you say? I can text you my address." Will smiled gently. "Say yes."

Ava looked like she was debating the proposition.

"You're not having any fun. That's why the hesitation, right?"

Ava laughed. "No. I'm having a great time. It's just… Madison claims you're a good guy, but John Wayne Gacy was a well-respected socialite, too. What's to say this isn't some ploy to get me in your basement dungeon?"

"While I just *love* to be compared to serial killers, you could always just text Madison before you come and have a set time for her to call you back. If you don't answer, she can call the cops."

She pressed her lips together and bobbed her head, doing her best Robert Deniro impression.

"I take it you watch a lotta true crime docs."

"Define *a lot*." Her laugh said it all.

"I never understood how people could watch that stuff."

"Dating is entirely different for a man than it is for a woman. For us, it can be downright terrifying. Only one percent of serial killers are women. Statistically speaking, men are the more dangerous of the sexes. The more we know, the more we can avoid becoming victims. For instance, if you saw someone walking around with a surfboard and a cast on their arm, would you help them if they struggle to load it?"

"With a cast? *Sure*."

"That's how Ted Bundy snatched two victims in one day."

Will adjusted uneasily in his chair. "That is definitely… *unnerving*."

"This isn't an ideal date conversation, is it?" She snickered and rubbed her forehead. "Sorry, I'm more than a little rusty."

"It's okay. You are the most stunning, interesting weirdo that I have met in… maybe ever."

She imagined lunging across the table to kiss him, hands gripping his shoulders, lips melding., hands wandering. She could practically taste his chapstick.

"So, million dollar question: are you looking for something casual or something… more?"

"Something more. I've tried casual. It's just not me. After my divorce, I wasn't quite sure who I was for a while. It took a while to figure out what I wanted and who *I* was." Ava absentmindedly finished the contents of her cup, set it back down, and turned her body fully toward Will in her seat. "I'm going to take a leap of faith that you aren't a cold-blooded murderer."

"If I was, I'd be *amazing* at the clean-up." He laughed.

Ava's lip twisted upward into a grin, and her eyebrows furrowed. "Boy, you are *really* convincing me."

Will shook his head, "I'm so sorry. It's not the time to make a joke. I see that now. You were saying?"

"I was *saying* I'm free Friday night."

He made a fist and jerked his elbow back to his side. "Yessss."

9

Thursday sped by like lightning for Ava. She spent the day dialing down her resume and qualifications and spraying it in every direction she could think of to get a half-decent job without having to leave Jackson Hole.

Friday brought giddiness all day as Ava debated her outfit and underwear set a thousand times, trying on nearly everything in her closet. She made a mental note to treat herself to some new clothes once she got new employment. She'd lost more weight than she'd realized after the divorce, and much of her apparel hung off her in a sloppy fashion.

Barely remembering to breathe properly for the drive across town, she finally arrived at the address Will texted her. She pulled up in front of a modest ranch-style house in the suburbs, piled beneath a foot of fresh, white powder. After another deep breath, she was outside, forging through the cold, crunching through the snow up the walkway.

Before she had the chance to knock, the door opened, revealing Will Jessup in a soft-looking baby-blue t-shirt that clung to his muscular physique and a pair of dark denim jeans. As Ava's eyes took him in from top to bottom, a laugh bubbled out of her. His socks were humorous, each peppered with pieces of pizza walking on legs, each with cartoon eyes.

"Nice." She pointed down to them, appreciating that the man had a sense of humor.

"Thank you. I figured they gave off less of a Bundy vibe." He gestured beyond a small, vaulted foyer. "Please, come in! Take off your coat. It's freezing out there."

"Thank you."

She entered, and he took her coat, whistling at the red dress beneath it, which hugged her delightfully curvaceous hips.

"My Lord." He bit his knuckle. "You are just… something else."

Ava felt red bloom through her cheeks.

"Come. Come. Welcome to *Cafe du Jessup*."

Though spotless, Will's home had a cozy feel. His house, smaller than most in the area, felt warm and full of life, filled with the scents of fresh coffee and lemon cleaner.

"How 'bout a quickie tour while the food I just pulled out of the oven cools?"

"Sure." Ava nodded, looking around.

Will waved her to the hallway, and she followed him down past several rooms extending off either side until the hallway came to a T. Ava wondered to herself how many women he had given the same tour to.

"Guest room." He gestured to his left and then moved to his right. "This one is my, like, I dunno what you'd call it… study? Office?"

Ava poked her head inside. Coffee-colored walls were dotted with nature photographs of local wildlife. A cushy, high-backed reading chair sat in one corner next to a tall bookcase loaded with paperbacks. A spotless desk with a small home computer took up the central space.

She followed Will further. He rapped a knuckle on one door.

"My room."

Ava felt the raptors claw at her stomach again and heat between her thighs. She wanted to see the room, to see if his bed was as she'd imagined…

"Forgive the mess. This one's Starla's room." He quickly swung open the door. The pink room was full of stuffed animals, piles of clothes, craft projects, and posters of unicorns. A hot pink canopy laced with string lights draped over an unmade bed. Will grimaced at the state of the room before shutting the door and leading Ava to the living room. He motioned to a plush couch with rich brown throw pillows on each side.

"And obviously, this is the living room. See? Small house. Told you it'd be a quick tour."

"It's beautiful."

"Thank you." He snatched the remote from the coffee table, which was an elevated wagon wheel topped with a thick, circular piece of glass. He flipped through TV apps until he found a video of a crackling fireplace. He placed the remote back on the table.

"I'll be back in a second with the food. Make yourself at home."

Ava nodded and walked in a slow circle around the room, soaking everything in. Eggshell-colored baseboards butted against creamy beige walls. Raw beams of oak ran along the length of the ceiling. Wrought iron sconces carried a warmth throughout. A beveled mirror hung beside the entrance to the kitchen. Black-and-white one-sheets from classic films adorned the walls, each in a large, uniquely-distressed frame. She studied all of the movie posters, arms clasped behind her back as if viewing works of art at a museum.

Wild Strawberries. Nosferatu. Dr. Strangelove. The Maltese Falcon…

All of them were originals, with fold marks carving them into squares throughout the image.

There were framed photos, too. Will and his daughter at the beach. Teenage Will, presumably at his high school graduation with his arms around what looked to be two proud parents. An infant swaddled in a unicorn blanket.

There were rustic figurines of black bears and elk along a thin table piled with opened mail. A rolled yoga mat tucked neatly beneath a decorative chair. Pink, tiny snow boots and jackets were neatly against the wall by the foyer. The small details gave the home warmth and a charm she hadn't expected. She worked her way back to the entertainment stand and eyed the rows of DVDs and Blu-rays. Some classics. Some children's movies. Many of the classics she'd seen before. Others looked unfamiliar. Some titles were even in different languages. None of the cases were still in the wrapping.

Will emerged from the kitchen with a platter of jalapeno poppers in one hand and red nuggets of something in the other. "I didn't know what you liked, so I made a few things. We have poppers and buffalo cauliflower bites. They taste like buffalo chicken but with a fraction of the calories." He set them down on the wagon wheel table. "Not that you need to watch your figure. I, however, do. No one wants big-ol' beer-gut Will to scrub their hot tub in fireman pants." He patted his abdomen, one Ava already knew had a chiseled six-pack. "I also have chicken nuggies because, let's face it, who doesn't like chicken nuggets?"

"I actually *love* chicken nuggets." Ava covered her smile.

"Yesssss. Good." Will pulled a fist down in the air. "And also coffee, which will be like a religious experience for you."

"Bring it on."

Will disappeared into the kitchen and returned with two steaming mugs of coffee and a plate of nuggets precariously balanced on his veiny forearm.

"Here, let me help." Ava jumped up to take the mugs, brushing his fingers gently with her own as she did. She smiled, nerves jangled, and sat on the couch. She patted the seat next to herself. He smiled as he sat.

"Try it. I love this brand." Will scooted her perfectly-foamed mug with its dash of cinnamon on top over to her.

"See, if you were a serial killer, this is how you'd drug me."

Will comically threw his hands up in the air. "Would you like me to take a sip first and show you that it's not been tinkered with?"

"Ewww, no." Ava paused for a moment and scrunched her face. "Cooties."

Will laughed, picked up his mug, and clanked it against hers. "Cheers, darling."

The pet name made Ava feel like a character out of one of the black-and-white films lining his media stand.

Ava took a sip, and her eyes grew wide. "Oh my God, Will. This is like Heaven in a cup!"

"Right? I told you. I don't play about my beans, man."

"Where do you get this stuff?"

"That's a secret. Can't divulge that information, unfortunately. Sorry. It's classified."

Ava laughed, grabbed a popper from the plate, and looked around. "Where's *Gremlin*?"

"Oh, she's probably asleep on my bed," Will called out over his shoulder. "Gremlin! Come here, girl!"

Silence.

"Gremlin, come on! You're makin' me look bad."

Still nothing.

Will mouthed to Ava, *I've got this.* "Fiiiiiine. More for us." Will smacked his lips as if enjoying some imaginary food.

Suddenly, the sound of nails clacking against wood floors rang out. Gremlin came screaming through the hall and through the living room. Losing traction, the pudgy pug skidded sideways and bowled all of her weight into Ava's calves. The motion wobbled her, dousing her dress with hot coffee.

"Shit!" She shrieked.

"Oh my God, Ava! Let me get you a towel!" Will leaped to his feet, slammed his mug on the table, and dashed into the kitchen. "I am so sorry!" he shouted.

"Holy shit… gah that burns!" Ava tore at the soaked-and-steaming fabric of her dress, fanning her lap. She stood and turned, pulling the skirt all the way up to fan her drenched panties.

"I'm so sorry!" Will shouted again as he scurried back with a couple of tea towels.

"It's okay. She didn't mean to do it."

Will handed the towels over her shoulder. Ava gingerly blotted her tender skin. Will dashed off again, returning a moment later from his bedroom. "Here. Here's a shirt and some sweatpants to change into. I'll go get you an icepack and some aloe gel for the burn."

"No, it's okay. I think the clothes will be fine." She held an arm out. He handed the clothes to her. "Can you… turn around?"

"Oh! Right. Right. Sorry." He made a face and turned, unaware that he'd been staring as she tore at her clothes.

At their feet, Gremlin lapped up a small puddle of spilled coffee from the floor.

Will caught the reflection of Ava stripping in the beveled mirror across from him. He tried to look away, but moments later, his eyes were studying the shape of her body, tracing the smooth skin that ran down her back to the dimples just above her lacy panties. He couldn't help but notice her bra and underwear matched, a good sign judging by his vast past experiences.

His heart rammed against his chest. Those weren't your everyday lounge-around-the-house underwear.

Those were panties you *wanted* to be seen.

His eyes were transfixed on the curves of her hips. The delicate definition of her shoulders. The shapeliness of her legs. He tried to scorch the image into his memory.

Hers was a body man fought to the death for. It deserved to be painted and hung in the finest gallery as art. Every inch cried out for his touch. His cock twitched in his pants, stiffening into the start of a problematic erection. He slid his idle hands over his lap to hide the rising tent there.

Now isn't the time, he thought silently, willing the tightness in his abdomen to dissipate.

She handed one of the towels back over her shoulder. "Can I have you wet this for me, please? The creamer's startin' to get sticky."

Her words anchored him back to reality. "Huh? Yes! *Wet* towel. Of course."

Frazzled, Will took it and hurried through his kitchen, one with dark wood grain, offset by stainless steel appliances and the warmth of amber pendant lights. Flicking his faucet to full blast, he ran the fabric beneath the water, accidentally hosing down the crotch of his pants with the wild spray in the process.

Pull it together, Will. Jesus, you act like you've never seen a woman's underwear before.

A part of him didn't want to listen, didn't want to pull it together at all. That part wanted to run his hands over her supple skin, tracing fingers over her shoulder and cup her breasts while he pressed into her from behind.

When he returned to the living room, Ava was pulling his sweatpants up over her underwear, already wearing his shirt. His eyes tracked to the way her nipples pressed against the fabric. It was then that he realized the shirt he'd given her read *'FBI: Female Body Inspector.'*

"Nice shirt." She chuckled, shaking her head. She reached out for the dampened tea towel. As he handed it over, their fingers grazed. Electric attraction, like a vibration on a cellular level, flowed between their skin.

"Sorry. I should have just shown you to the bathroom. I don't know what I was thinking," Will said, running a hand through his sandy hair.

"It's alright." She turned around again, pulling his T-shirt away from her skin to wipe down her breasts and stomach to remove the stickiness from her agitated skin.

"I will say," she laughed, "I've never had someone get me out of my clothes that early into a date."

"I'd like to say I'm honored or make a joke right now, but I know you're in pain." Will raced into the bathroom for a moment and retrieved a small container of aloe vera gel, handing it to Ava upon his return.

She poured a small amount on her hand and rubbed it against the tender skin of her chest, cooling her burns. "Thank you."

She pulled the shirt down over her gelled skin and turned to face Will. Will lowered to the floor and wiped up the wet Gremlin-sized paw prints.

Will gave the pug a quick kiss on the snout. Gremlin snorted.

"Are you alright," Will asked as he stood.

"I'm fine."

Will gathered her dress and bra in one fell scoop and nodded at the couch. "Have a seat in the burn ward. I'll get your dress in a bag. I'll pay for the dry cleaning."

"Oh, you don't have to do—"

"Nonsense. It's the least I can do."

"I'll make you a fresh cup while I am at it. Feel free to eat while the other stuff is still hot."

Will's smile was bright and bold, stunning Ava into momentary silence.

He disappeared around the corner again and headed to the trashcan. Without thinking, he stepped on the pedal and threw the clothes in. "Damn it." Half a second later, he mashed the pedal again and pulled them out, flustered. "What am I doing?"

You gotta calm down, man. Pull it together! So what if you can see her nipples through your t-shirt? So what if the image of her drenched, lacy panties is seared into your brain? You're done with flings, remember? You have a shot at something real this time. Don't blow this!

Will shoved the dress into a grocery bag and set it on the counter. He hurriedly returned to the living room. "If it's alright with you, I have a movie in mind for us."

"Oh yeah? What movie?"

"Ever seen *An Affair to Remember?*"

She thought for a moment. "No."

"Well, I think you'd like it. It's like a more romantic version of *Sleepless in Seattle*, in my opinion."

"Ooooh, I love that one," she admitted, popping a cauliflower bite into her mouth and settling back into the lush couch. "I've heard about that one, but I've never seen it."

"Great! I think you'll like this one a lot. Something about this movie is just timeless and pure." Will took a seat beside her.

"Oh my God." Ava reeled back in amazement. "I say the same thing about *Casablanca* all the time."

They looked at each other for a beat too long, tendrils of attraction tugging them together like a giddy octopus. Will scooted closer until they were both sitting in the middle of the couch, legs gently touching, feeling the low buzz of electricity course through the point of contact.

He pushed play, traded the remote for a chicken nugget, and leaned back into the couch beside her. Effortlessly, he took her hand and interlaced their fingers together, resting them on her sweatpants-covered leg. As the opening credits began, they nestled next to one another and tried to ignore the undeniable attraction, pulling their focus from the screen.

＊＊＊

At some point in the third act, Will realized Ava hadn't stirred in a while. He glanced down. She was laid against his arm, head slumped onto his shoulder, eyes shut, breathing rhythmically. He watched her sleep for a moment and felt the strangest feelings…

Contentment.

Joy.

He wanted to live in that moment for eternity, feeling her against him, appreciating the trust that comes with falling asleep beside someone. He imagined her green eyes opening in the morning. He tried to picture how captivating she must look with tousled hair framing her groggy features.

He swept a dangling strand of red-brown hair from her face, tucking it softly behind her ear. The gesture was just enough to wake her. Ava batted open her eyes and gasped quietly.

"Oh, God, I'm so sorry." She chuckled. "Did I drool on you?"

Will snorted. "No. No drool. You're okay."

Ava rubbed her hands over her face and up through her hair. "I haven't slept that good in *months*."

"So… it was a *riveting* date then?"

"Oh my God, I didn't mean it like that. No, actually… it was wonderful."

"I'm glad. I guess if you could doze off like that, you decided I'm not a serial killer?"

"*Jury's still out*," she teased with narrowed eyes.

They stared at one another in silence, heads propped against the backrest of the couch. Will felt a strong urge to kiss her. Ava felt it, too, as if his lips were beckoning her like the song of a siren.

"This was so nice." Will took a deep breath, stood from the couch, and gathered the empty platters from the table. "I promise to have your dress dry-cleaned in time for our next date."

"Oh," Ava rose, silently cursing herself for whatever she did to spook him from going in for the kiss. "So, you think there will be a *next* date, huh?" She asked, hands on her hips, unaware her bra-less breasts were pressing through the fabric.

It took every ounce of focus for Will to maintain eye contact and smile with confidence. "Why, yes, I do."

She smiled and headed to the foyer, bundling up in her long coat. "I have an idea in mind for the next one that's *guaranteed* to keep me awake."

"Alright. Text me when and where. I'll be there." Will returned from the kitchen and met her at the front door, Gremlin trotting close behind.

She gave Gremlin a goodbye scratch on the head. "This was fun."

"I had a good time, too." Will maneuvered ahead of her and opened the front door. He gazed into her eyes for a moment before quietly muttering, "I really want to kiss you right now, but I'm trying to be a good boy."

Ava's eyes glittered in the sodium vapor streetlight bathing the snow all around them in its orange hue. She fought the urge to grin. "Okay. Well, don't be a good boy for too long."

Will struggled to find the words, exhaling a frosty breath up against the door jamb above them. "I have made a lot of mistakes in my past. I've jumped the gun. Gone off and ruined things before they could properly start." His eyes gazed at her with sincerity. "I'm trying to do things right this time."

Ava nodded, wordless and filled with respect at the display of self-control. It was a compliment of the highest order. "Goodnight, Will."

"Goodnight."

Ava trudged through the high snow toward her SUV, tightening her coat to ward away the bristling wind. Will felt a hand grasp his heart and squeeze. When she got to her vehicle, she cast a glance back over her shoulder, and he waved. At that moment, they both exchanged the same forlorn look.

Neither one wanted Ava to go.

10

That night, Ava lay awake, staring at the empty half of her king-sized bed. She draped her arm across the cool pillow and pulled it to her chest. She had never *once* regretted kicking out her ex-husband after finding out about the affair.

It wasn't much of a marriage to *begin* with.

Dan's scent was long gone from her bedding, it having been laundered many times since. But no amount of fabric softener in the world washed away the terrible memories. The loneliness. The feeling of not being enough. The feeling of not being someone's whole world.

Memories flashed through her mind with the 20/20 clarity of hindsight. Every phony smile, every faked orgasm, every late-night shower, every kiss... all of it was a damned *lie*. A beautifully curated fallacy she'd orchestrated throughout the years to quell the distrust, all to soothe herself for obviously settling. She could recognize now, in retrospect, that she'd turned a blind eye to every red flag, every sign. Suspicions were blanketed over by a forced, blind trust in someone who lied in front of God and their families that he would love and cherish, honor, and be faithful. From the shadows, reality had slapped her in the face with its cold, lesson-riddled hand.

…Lessons she hadn't been ready for.

Her mind played back an ugly highlight reel of painful memories. Perfume on his work clothes. Car seats pushed too far forward. Late-night texts from the office. Strange charges on the account. The rumors at the Christmas party. The marks on his back that looked suspiciously like nail drags.

It had all been lies. Every last moment of their sham marriage.

Did he ever love me, she wondered?

Was there ever a time when the care he showed was real?

During their final blowout, he'd broken down and told her about the affairs. *Plural.* Ava foolishly recalled thinking they could work through it, using honesty as a foundation to rebuild their twister-ravaged vows.

That was until he told her that his current something-on-the-side was *pregnant.*

Every time Ava thought back to it, her chest ached. Not because of the unfaithful idiot she had married. It ached for the fact that Dan was about to have the family *she'd always dreamed of having.*

She thought the divorce had absolutely broken her. She wasn't looking for someone. Nor did she ever think she would want more than a casual fling ever again.

She tossed and turned, finally settling on the empty pillow, and tried to imagine Will Jessup laying in bed beside her, caressing the hair from her cheek just as he had tonight when she was teetering on the edge of a dream.

All instincts of self-preservation had been tossed out the window, and a singular, haunting realization had taken their place…

Will was in her head.

$$\|\|$$

The light of dawn peeked through the blinds of Will's kitchen windows. An early riser, he always awoke before the sun, stumbling to the countertop cappuccino machine for a sip of caffeinated lifeblood. Making coffee was an art he'd nearly perfected, even with his eyes only half-open. His tousled hair bobbed softly as he worked. He tamped grounds down into the Port-a-filter, readied it in its slot, and flicked the switch. The machine *whooshed* to life.

On autopilot, he poured some milk into a metal carafe and placed it under the steam valve. He twisted the side dial. Milk bubbled inside. Will filled his coffee mug and artfully drizzled foamy white milk on top of the black espresso, creating a cappuccino that would put most coffee shops to shame.

Golden sunlight beamed into his eyes from between the slats of his blinds, eliciting a grumble. He took a sip of the steaming liquid, and his shoulders relaxed, letting out a small groan of pleasure. He felt revived, as though he had suddenly returned to the living after having been dead.

He missed his partner in crime. Soon, Starla would wake from her sleepover and call him to come and pick her up. But, for now, the silence invading his home made him feel uneasy. He was used to ridiculous inquiries and off-the-wall conversations with her first thing in the morning. The *"but why?"* question after everything had become part of their morning ritual.

Every day with her was both exhausting and rewarding. He swore he was going to raise Starla differently than *he'd* been reared. She would never feel like a burden, something to simply be *endured*. No. He wanted his child to know she was cherished from day one. And though he was far from perfect, he felt like he'd done a good job of that so far. He'd always provided for her, never letting her see how close their ship had come to sinking.

Silence had vanished the day Starla was born, and it went surprisingly *unmissed*. This morning, it had returned with a vengeance, and now he was excited for his little girl's peppy antics, ranging from begging for 'bunny pancakes' to prodding for a satisfactory answer to 'which dinosaur would he be able to beat in a fight?' As his daughter blossomed into a social butterfly at school, he both loved and hated the times when Starla would stay then night at other kid's houses. It was both a sacred time of peace and contemplation… and a ringing reminder that there was no romance in his life, no one to share his mind and soul with.

His days were a pink, frilly whirlwind full of girly stuffed animals, dog hair, and laughter. Yet, in the back of his mind, he couldn't seem to shake the feeling that it was all still *missing* something.

For months after Sarah left, Will went on a tear, sleeping with countless women, ones all too willing to be teased and pleased. Ones whose last name he rarely caught. Back when he was a single father of a toddler, he didn't have much time for romance. Only sex to fill the void, to fill the emptiness.

He silently sipped his cappuccino, and his eyes drifted to the mug in the sink that his would soon be joining.

Ava's cup.

A valiant ceramic hero who got Ava (at least mostly) naked. He thought back to that moment, replaying it in his mind. He recalled the line her bra left in her milky skin when she'd removed it. He'd desperately wanted to run his fingers along the impressions, caressing the smooth flesh in the grooves. The thought reawakened his morning erection, which stood bolt-upright, puffing his flannel pajama bottoms out like a boat sail in gale-force winds.

He sighed in frustration.

Ugh. There was no one to share *that* with either.

12

Will scrubbed at a ring around a jetted Jacuzzi. Today's uniform was a pair of tuxedo budgie-smugglers, a fire-engine red bow tie, and shirt cuffs sans sleeves. *The ChippenMale Dancer,* as he called the outfit on his website, to avoid a copyright infringement suit.

In a town chock full of lawyers, he could never be too careful.

His bare chest flexed as he scrubbed on hands and knees, giving Carla O'Neil an unimpeded view of his spandex-covered ass.

She sat on the edge of the tub, sneaking glances and looking away again, cheeks pink with embarrassment. Her voluptuous form tugged at the buttons of her blouse. Her stretchy slacks were more taut than he remembered. The Tuscan-style bathroom, with beige walls and pale brown tile, bathed her in a golden hue. The favorable light softened her striking features into those of a cherub statue in a museum.

"She said Vicky told her that *I said* she was allegedly a slut, which is not true. That's not something I would ever say. I wouldn't slut-shame someone like that. It's not in my nature. I'm very sex-positive." Her soft, excited tone made Will smile. He couldn't tell if she always spoke so much because she was nervous or if she was simply lonely.

"Of course. In my experience, that's not at all like you." He stopped scrubbing for a moment and addressed her over his muscular shoulder. "You stood up for yourself, right? I hope you gave her a piece of your mind."

Her eyes drifted to the floor, embarrassed. Her shoulders slumped.

"It's okay, Mrs. O'Neil. Don't beat yourself up over it. It sounds like they don't know you at all. And that's *their* loss." He resumed scrubbing.

"That's what I was thinking," she shouted with a wince. She spoke again, quieter. "I'm sorry. That was so loud—"

"*Frankly, dear, I don't give a damn,*" he said in his best Rhett Butler impression. "No more apologizing for little stuff like that. Be who you are. Don't let people force you into some little box. This is your house. If you wanna be loud, girl... be *loud*." He rinsed his sponge under the faucet. "You are allowed to take up space in this world. You're allowed to speak your mind. You're allowed to exist freely. People can like it, or they can kick rocks. That's *their* problem. Not yours. Remember, *nobody puts baby in the corner*."

She snickered, but Will could see a hint of sadness in her smile. "You're sweet. Thank you for listening. I know I talk your ear off when you're over here."

"I'm always happy to listen." Will stood, abdomen rippling, and positioned himself on his knees at the other end of the large Jacuzzi to scour the other half. "We, as humans, need to be good to one another. And I, myself, have always depended on the kindness of strangers."

"Gone with the Wind?"

"Streetcar Named Desire. But not a bad guess." Will wiped the sweat beading on his forehead with a cuffed forearm. "Is it hot in here to you?"

"I probably have the central heat cranked too high. I can go turn it down."

"No. Please don't trouble yourself. I'm almost done."

Carla rolled up the sleeves of her blouse, feeling heat rise from beneath her buttoned collar as she watched his glorious body hard at work. "You always make me forget what I'm talking about when you get scrubbing like that." A smile crept onto her full cheeks. "That little tuxedo get-up looks good on you."

"Thank you. I had to special order it. I'm glad you approve."

"I think it's my new favorite." She giggled. "I need to get you some of those underwear in every color."

Will stopped scrubbing. His eyes followed the bruised flesh of her forearm up to a marking that looked eerily similar to a partial handprint.

She followed his gaze and quickly pulled her sleeves back down. "That's why they call me 'Clumsy Carla,' always showing up with some new bruise," she muttered unconvincingly.

Will set the sponge down in the bottom of the tub before leaning back on his heels to face her. "Did you put that dent in the pantry door with your fist, too?"

Silence filled the room for a moment as Carla thought of a believable excuse. "I tripped over a bag of groceries. I tried to catch myself but ended up putting a hand almost straight through the darned thing. Pfft. *Only clumsy Carla.*" She shook her head and swallowed hard, praying he believed her.

The disappointed look he offered said he knew she was lying.

Her shoulders sank further with defeat. "It's fine. Just leave it."

"You know you don't have to stay, right? There are places you can go. Shelters. A friend's house. A hotel. I could take you myself if you need a ride."

Her eyebrows shifted, her face morphing into an angry expression. "Are you kidding? Look around, Mr. Jessup. You see this house. Look at me. Hair styled. Nails manicured. Expensive clothes. Financially, I'm set for life. My *kids* are set. They have a life I could never even *dream* of as a child. Do you think I could give them this kind of life on my own? I don't even have a high school diploma."

"Money isn't everything, Mrs. O'Neil." Will shook his head, frustrated. "Money doesn't give people like your husband the right to hurt the people he is supposed to protect."

"He does love me. And he *adores* the kids. He'd never hurt them."

"You sure about that?" Will growled.

"Trust me, Will. I'm no saint. I can be infuriating. My mama always said I could make a preacher swear."

"Oh, come on," he grabbed her hand, "no woman deserves that, Carla. I don't care what the circumstances. There's no excuse whatsoever."

She pulled her hand away and stood, crossing her arms defensively. "When things are good, they're *so* good. The bad times are much more rare. That's what marriage is. Through the good times *and* the bad, that's what our vows said. He's made some mistakes. We all have. He's just stressed out with work right now."

Will didn't believe that this abuse was some sort of recent development. In fact, she wore long sleeves in the summertime, too, which always struck him as odd.

Now, it all made sense.

"I get that this isn't an easy decision for you, but please consider what I said. When you're ready, I'll happily be the one to take you wherever you need to go."

She smiled weakly. "Thank you."

Will nodded and looked around, trying to figure out what part of the already clean bathroom to pretend to scrub next.

"You won't tell any of the other ladies, will you? You know how they like to talk."

"No." Will shook his head. "That's your business. I'd never gossip like that or betray someone's confidence."

He knew now was not the time to push her. Now was the time to let his offer marinate. All he could do was hope.

He walked over to the mirror and hosed it down with blue glass spray. He pulled off some paper towels and started wiping, changing the subject as his thighs flexed to reach the higher spots. He watched in the reflection as Carla's eyes locked back onto his body. "How's Laura?"

"Oh, that daughter of mine's gonna put me into an early grave. I swear, she is nothing like I was when I was her age."

"Well, thankfully, she has a strong female role model to help guide her."

Will let the words sink in, not saying anything more.

In the silence was the realization that Carla was, in fact, an example for her daughter. In the right ways…

And the *wrong*.

At that moment, fully dressed, she suddenly felt far more exposed, naked, and vulnerable than the man in front of her, wearing little more than a bow tie.

13

"Okay, so what is this date? Why was I supposed to bundle up?" Will asked, rubbing his chilled hands together through his thick fleece gloves.

The wind had finally settled for once. The town was quiet. Smoke whirled its way up from chimneys, drifting and dissipating like wayward ghosts in the night air. The cloudy sky threatened to open up on them. Even in the dim moonlight, he was drawn to Ava's beauty.

A pink hue had kissed her cheeks and her nose. Her hair was down in bouncy waves. Light makeup accentuated her features. Her lipstick drew his eyes to her enticing mouth.

"We are almost at the first stop." She skipped ahead, bare legs peeking out from beneath the hem of her coat, just above her completely impractical boots. She eyed him over her shoulder, driving him crazy with those glimmering eyes. Every time they landed on him, he felt himself melt beneath their warm gaze.

"First stop?"

"Just go with it."

Will shrugged. "Alright. I'll bite."

Will followed her into the back door of an intimate, dim bar with a few booths lining the walls. Rustic dark wood walls flowed into a hardwood floor. Gray beams ran up the corners and along the elevated roof. Country music played softly, muffled by the mumble of the scarce patrons within the establishment. Each table seemed isolated, contained in some invisible capsule that separated them from the outside world. Ava took a seat in an unoccupied booth, and Will slid across from her.

Ava shrugged off her jacket, revealing a black cowl-neck top with shoulder cutouts. The fabric gracefully draped along her arms and cinched again to the cuff of fabric at her wrists. Her dangling earrings hung low, just above her shoulders, glittering like her eyes in the overhead lights.

"This is my treat this time. Consider it my penance for falling asleep on you during the movie."

"Blasphemy," he joked. "Just kidding. It was actually quite adorable."

Ava shied away from his sincere gaze. "Well, thank you."

"It's true. It's also adorable how easily you get embarrassed. You're blushing."

"Would you *stop*?" She waved him away. "Big deal. I blush. I bet I could make you blush, too."

"I'd love to see you try." He leaned back. "Not much embarrasses me these days. Scrubbing floors in front of a bunch of women in nothing but a banana hammock desensitizes you a bit."

"I'll make those cheeks rosy. Just watch." She grinned, wondering where her sudden brazen confidence had surfaced from. She secretly blamed it on the lace thong she had on, reserved for special occasions.

A waiter approached, his puff of curls bouncing atop his head. His eyes were bloodshot, and the odor of marijuana said he was at least a blunt deep into his evening. "Welcome to Drexel's. What can I get you tonight?"

Ava started. "I'll have a—"

"Lemon drop martini?" Will grinned.

"You remembered?" Ava grinned.

"Only the important stuff." He looked up at the young kid. "I'll have an old-fashioned, please."

"Got it." The waiter jotted down, tucking the pen back into the curls behind his ear. He strolled away, leaving the faint air of weed in his wake.

"You know, this is the second bar you have taken me to in two dates. I think you have a problem," Will teased.

"It's just the first stop. I thought you might not be thrilled to be walking around out in the cold for our date. Figured maybe a little booze could help keep us warm."

"You know, alcohol *thins* the blood. It doesn't actually raise your body temperature. It actually makes you more prone to hypothermia—"

"Wow. Someone is a know-it-all."

"Learned that in my first year of nursing school." Will chuckled and leaned back into the cushioned seat. The breadth of his shoulders and the tilt of his chin felt powerful. He took up his entire side of the booth, stretching out his muscular arms.

"That was before my days as a man-maid."

"Still feels weird calling you that."

"People could call me a *chicken wrangler* for all I care. A title is just a title. A job is just a job. It's not an *identity*."

"I was embarrassed to tell people I was a Chief Revenue Officer. Mostly because nobody knew what it was."

"Chief Revenue Officer, huh? Sounds," he struggled for the right term, "I don't know. Frankly, it sounds very boring."

"Oh God, yes. So much red tape, paperwork, coordinating people… schmoozing clients I didn't like. I wasn't even a *cog* in a machine. I was a *tine of a cog* in a machine. Big title, big paycheck, big responsibility, lots of travel… and in the end, it meant nothing. None of it was as tangible as what you do. When you clean a room, you can stand back and *see* your efforts. You made something better in this world, even if only temporarily. Mine was all theoretical. Just a ten-year blur of numbers and graphs."

"That may be, but you got a beautiful house out of it. I've seen it."

"True. And… it's almost paid off. Fortunately, I have a nice little nest egg to fall back on as well. So I am in a good position to figure out what it is I really want to do."

"Might I suggest being a maid?" He laughed. "It's very fulfilling."

"As you well know, I am not the clean type."

"What?! You? Noooo," he teased.

"Although that chicken wrangler thing you mentioned sounds like it could be fun." She threw her cocktail napkin at him as the waiter came back with their drinks.

"Here you are." With the precision and focus of someone working on a nuclear bomb, the waiter's bloodshot eyes stared intently as he set each drink down in front of the wrong person.

"Thanks," Will said with a nod.

As soon as the waiter walked away, they swapped their beverages. Will picked up his old-fashioned and smelled the sweet blend of alcohol and muddled fruit. Ava examined his drink. A neat ball of ice floated in the center of a pool of amber liquid, the rim decorated with a slice of orange.

"I never had an old-fashioned. Are they any good?"

Will took a sip. "They're amazing. This one is pretty good. Would you like to try it?"

Ava nodded, eagerly drawing it to her face. "Smells like whiskey."

"It is."

"Ah." Ava took a sip and stopped cold. She grimaced, unsure what to do with the tingling bitter liquid.

He stared at her intently, an upturn in the corners of his lips. He could see it written in the creases of her eyes.

She hated it.

She forced herself to swallow it. She tried to smile, mouth warped with regret and discomfort. The potent mix scorched its way down her throat. She exhaled what felt like fire. "Gah! That's.... *Bleh*!"

"Pretty sure I would react the same with a sip of *yours*." He made a face at her martini.

"Mine tastes like sunshine and candy. Yours tastes like lighter fluid and fruit."

He shook his head and took a long sip of his cocktail. Something about his eye contact and serious expression turned her on.

She took a swallow of her martini to combat the disgust and slid it over to him.

"No, thanks."

"If you like sweet things, you'll love this. Trust me."

"No self-respecting man would be caught dead with a drink like that in public."

"News flash: nobody gives a shit about that kind of gender crap anymore."

"Are you trying to get me drunk? *Mrs. Robinson, you're trying to seduce me, aren't you?*"

She raised an eyebrow at that. "Would I even need to get you drunk to do that? Women talk, you know. Your reputation precedes you."

"*Madison.*" He shook his head, a little embarrassed.

"Love the girl, but she *always* spills the tea."

"Ah, well, what can I really say? Yeah, I should just be straight with you."

Ava sipped her martini, eyes never leaving his.

"I had my fun. After Sarah and I split, I went on a bit of a spree." He shrugged and swirled the ball of ice in his glass. "Got a bit of a reputation, but I also got that wildness out of my system. But there was one night I decided… enough, you know? I had to change some things."

"One night? What happened?"

"Well, talking about this kinda stuff is not really good date conversation."

"On the contrary. Dating is how we are supposed to get to know this stuff about each other to find out if we want to keep investing time and effort into each other."

"Mmm. I see your point. You sure you wanna hear this?"

"Positive."

He pinched the bridge of his nose. "Starla, my little girl, her blood sugars spiked while she was at a sleepover. One of the parents didn't know she was diabetic, and they ordered pineapple pizza and drank punch."

"Disgusting." Ava feigned gagging. "The pineapple on pizza part, I mean."

"*Agreed*." Will pointed to her and then fondled his glass again. "She's a little self-conscious about her illness and how it makes her different from other kids, so she was too shy to say anything. When she checked her numbers afterward, they were sky-high. She went to the girl's dad and showed him, and he freaked. Started calling me over and over. Across town, I was in the middle of… *um*… *it.* My phone was across the room. I didn't hear it for like an hour."

"Oh…"

He rubbed his lips, struggling to keep the emotion out of his voice. "She could have died. She had to go to the hospital so doctors could intervene. I wasn't there when she needed me."

Ava's eyes dropped to her martini for a moment. It was hard to watch him chastise himself for being a human with needs and desires.

"I wasn't thinking." He cleared his throat again, hoping to swallow the lump that had arisen. "I was so busy trying to get laid instead of being a dad. It was selfish. I don't want to be that guy. I'm looking for something *more* now, anyway."

Ava suddenly felt empathetic, "You really seem to care about your daughter. She's very lucky to have you."

"I'm the lucky one." He took a swallow of his drink and smacked his lips. "Ah, so, you've heard some of my drama. Now, I want some of yours."

"Like what? I'm an open book."

"So, how long ago did you and your ex… *husband*…?" He fished to see if he was correct.

"Yes," she nodded, "ex-husband."

"How long ago was your split?"

She looked up at the light as if to calculate. "The divorce was finalized… just about six months ago."

"Why did you guys split? If you don't mind my asking." The dangling light over the booth illuminated the closely-shorn stubble on his face, bathing him in delicious honey-colored light.

"Oh, you know that old story… boy meets girl. Boy marries girl. Girl finds out she's infertile. Boy stops touching girl. Boy starts touching every girl but his girl. Boy knocks up his secretary. Girl finds pregnancy test in her kitchen trash can."

"Wow." His eyes were large.

She laughed through the pain in her gut. "She just had the baby last week."

Will sat stunned across the table, scrambling for something to say. "I'm so sorry I even asked."

"Nah, don't be." She waved him off. "I'm not. Single best decision I ever made. We were *miserable* together."

"Sounds like you landed on your feet."

"I landed on my face… I get knocked down, but I get up again—"

"*Neva' gonna keep me down,*" Will finished the lyrics.

Ava clapped quietly. "Encore!"

Will smirked and pretended to curtsy in his seat.

A comfortable silence passed between them as they looked into each other's eyes. To Ava, his blue eyes felt like… home. She couldn't explain it. She had the urge to touch him, to caress him. Every cell of her being screamed for her to lean across the table and kiss him. She pictured their lips pressed against one another, his hungry tongue exploring the depths of her mouth, manly hands in her hair, eagerly pulling her closer…

Ava didn't dare to tell him his crystal-blue eyes felt like peering into glacial waters she wanted to endlessly swim in. She licked the rim of her martini glass, and Will's mind drifted, imagining what the inside of her mouth would feel like wrapped around him.

Will cleared his throat and shifted in his seat. "Penny for your thoughts."

"You have a really kind, disarming smile."

"Thanks. I appreciate it." He tossed back the last swig of his drink. "So… where to after this?"

"You'll see." Ava smiled and tossed some money down on the table for the tab. She put on her coat and thick gloves. "Bundle up."

***

"*An ice rink?*"

"Yup!" Ava's high-heeled, impractical boots crunched into the drift against the building, choosing the grip of snow over the slick ice of the walkway.

"You should come over here and walk on this slick-ass sidewalk with me so I have an excuse to hold your hand," Will hollered, arms jutting out for balance on the icy path.

She clomped through the snow like a newborn elk and snagged his hand mid-air, weaving her fingers through his. "You don't have to have an excuse."

"This is gonna be *rough*."

"Oh, come on," Ava teased. "What's a good date without a few injuries?"

Ava dug in her purse and produced two five-dollar bills, placing them on the chilled wooden counter of the skate rental shack.

"What size?" the teenage girl asked.

"I need a pair of size nines," Ava chirped.

Will stood up straight. "Can I get a size nine, too, please?"

Ava smirked and pretended to zipper her lips. "I have the tact to say nothing."

The attendant handed over two identical pairs of skates.

Will seemed unfazed. "Thanks."

They carefully stepped over to an unoccupied bench to put on their footwear.

Ava chuckled. "I'm sorry, but I have never dated a guy with the same size feet as me."

"Well, it can't be easy being a girl with such big feet?"

"I don't have big feet! You have small feet. Size nine is *tiny* for a man."

"You know what they say about men with little feet?"

Ava only stared at him, lacing her skates.

"Little *shoes*." He laughed and stood on his skates like a wobbly giraffe. "Good Lord, I've never done this before. Please tell me you are good at this."

"Yeah," Ava said, tying the lace of the second skate into a knot. "I am alright."

"Good, because I need somebody to keep me from breaking both my legs at this!"

Ava made her way gracefully to the ice with no wobble to her stride. She turned back and extended a hand to him as she arrived at the gate. On quivering legs, he made his way toward her. He leaned out to clasp her hand and used it to steady himself.

"Look at you! Ms. Ice Castles over here. You are just *full* of surprises."

"Why, thank you."

"Promise me, Ava, if I die this way, you'll tell my daughter I died in, like, a *way* cooler way. Tell her I was eaten by a bobcat… or lost a brawl. Something *manly*."

Ava led him slowly onto the ice. Other skaters circled around as Will struggled to stay upright, grabbing onto the side rail for stability. Ava skated backward.

"Of course, you can skate backward. You make it look so easy!"

Ava held out her hands and smiled, the tip of her nose rosy. "You got this. Come to me. I'll pull you for a bit until you get used to it."

Stiff-legged and rigid, Will's skates met the shallow grooves in the ice left by those before him, and he scuttled forward awkwardly until his gloved hands were in hers.

"See? You got this." Ava teased, releasing his hands.

Several small children bundled up in puffy jackets whizzed past them.

"*Pfft*, show offs!" Will hollered.

Ava chuckled, gently dragging him along, legs weaving with skill and precision. "See how I'm moving my legs?"

"Like a snake?"

"Yeah, try it."

With unsteady knees and rubbery ankles, Will attempted an awkward weave, mimicking Ava's movements to the best of his ability.

"How are you so *good* at this?!"

"I played hockey for a little bit in high school. I loved being on the ice, but I got knocked *hard* into a wall during a game. Got a really bad concussion. Parents pulled me out after that."

"A concussion? That explains a lot," Will teased.

"Wow. What's that? You wanna skate on your *own*?" She let his hands go and skated backward away from him.

Will flailed, laughing "What? Wait a minute! No! Come back here!"

"Remember, weave, don't walk." Ava whooshed ahead, skated back, and executed a quick hockey stop, showering him in shaved ice.

"Hey!" Shouted the skate attendant, yelling to get Ava's attention. He shook his head, knitting his eyebrows together, his lips pressed into a flat line. He wagged a finger at her as if scolding a naughty puppy.

Ava held up a hand. "Sorry!"

Will's skates slid out in front of him. "Shit!" He grabbed the side rail to keep from falling.

"It's alright. You got it. Just stay close to the wall and grab on when you think you are gonna fall. It will help you gain your balance."

Will pulled himself along, lapped by small children who were chasing each other across the ice.

"Alright. I think I am getting it. How's this?" He wove his feet slowly, fighting to keep his eyes off of his skates.

"Eyes up. Look at me, not the ground, okay?" Ava bellowed.

"Like this?"

"Yeah, you're doing it!" She rejoiced, watching the smile fall from Will's face all of a sudden.

"*Ava, look out!*"

The second that Ava turned to look, a skater slammed into her full force. Both legs slid out from under her, sending her smashing into the ice face-first.

"Oh God. Ava!" Will pushed himself away from the wall and used the momentum to skitter toward her.

***

"Well, this is… embarrassing," Ava croaked as she held the cobbled-together excuse for an ice pack to her injured nose. Will had made her one on the fly with an old peanut butter and jelly sandwich Ziploc bag Starla left in the door's pocket packed with fresh snow from the parking lot. Ava soaked up the warmth from his heating vents and subtly looked around. The interior of Will's truck was recently detailed and smelled like the new sandalwood air freshener that hung from the rearview.

"Don't be embarrassed. Who cares that you biffed it? In *spectacular* fashion, I might add. I mean, Ava… you *caught air*. You're like a superhero. I wasn't aware you could *fly*."

Ava chuckled, voice nasally through the cold pack. "One of my *many* talents."

"Doesn't look like you broke anything or need stitches. It could have been way worse. But, you may end up with a black eye or two."

"Eh, that's fine. It's not like they're going to ask me about it at my *job* tomorrow." She scoffed and returned her green eyes to him. "Just a bummer. After this, I was gonna take you to see *Harvey* at the little theater near my house. They're doing a 35mm screening of it."

"Yeah? I love that one. I tried to get Starla to name her stuffed rabbit Harvey."

"No, you did not!" Ava laughed.

"Oh yeah. But she insisted on another equally dumb name."

"That's funny." Ava sighed, slumping a little with defeat. "Yeah. I was gonna invite you back for a coffee at my place after the screening.

I don't have a fancy coffee maker or imported stuff like you—"

"Oh?" His mind ping-ponged between the thought of going back to her home and what he would do to her body if given the chance. His thoughts drifted to fantasies of kissing her neck. Cupping those bare breasts. Trailing fingers down her stomach…

He refocused his eyes on the injured woman in front of him. "One time on a date, I ate something that didn't agree with my stomach. We started driving down this washboard back road—"

Ava pulled the cluster of napkins away from her nose and chuckled. "What? You *sharted* or or something?"

"No." He chuckled. "Thank God. But I threw up."

Ava laughed. "Okay, that's worse than a bloodied nose, I think."

"Oh, no. Just wait. It gets better." Will grabbed a fresh napkin from inside the bench between them and softly dabbed at the fresh drop of blood beneath her nose with care. "I didn't have time to get out of the truck. I threw up on the dash."

"Ewwww."

"And as I skidded to a stop, it all came rushing back at us."

Ava closed her eyes, battling not to laugh right in his face but losing miserably.

He paused for a moment to touch her cheek, taking in her bright, beautiful smile, tousled hair still a disheveled mess. *He'd never wanted to kiss someone so bad in his life.*

But he was serious about doing things differently this time. He'd made a promise to himself. He wasn't about to break it.

As if she could tell what he was thinking, she leaned into his hand, laughter abating, rubbing against the soft flesh of his palm, staring back into his eyes for a moment that was nearly perfect.

It took every cell of Will's body to pull his hand away. "I guess we should probably get you home so you can tend to these wounds."

"We probably should." Ava was taken aback. Despite the catastrophe, she'd secretly held out hope he would come home with her.

After all, this was their *third* date, the one to be traditionally rumored to be the night where even a well-mannered gentleman makes his move.

Ava removed the MacGyvered ice pack from her face and looked down at the blood stain on her coat. "Oh no. Dammit. I *loved* this coat."

"The easiest solution is cold water and soap. Just scrub, scrub, scrub. Hydrogen peroxide, in my opinion, doesn't work as well, especially on colors. You can end up doing more harm than good."

Ava smiled. "I love that you're a stain expert."

"Occupational hazard." He breathed deeply, fogging up the truck windows. "Let me walk you back to your car."

Ava nodded without a word, trying to hide her disappointment. As they arrived at her black SUV, she spoke. "Thank you for coming tonight. I'm sorry about… all this." She pointed to her nose, pink from injury and pale in spots from the cold, and then fiddled nervously with her keys. She got inside, started the vehicle, and rolled down the window.

He leaned in, pressing his forearms to the door. "Wanna do this again sometime? Maybe something without so much blood?"

She snickered. "I'd like that."

"Me too."

Ava looked up at him, heart thundering in her chest, stomach fluttering with a potent mixture of excitement and jangled nerves.

"Okay. I'll text you tomorrow. Drive safe." Will patted the side of her SUV gently and turned away.

As Ava drove away, wheels crunching through snow and black ice, all she could wonder was where she had gone wrong and what she'd done to make him not want to *at least kiss her*.

14

Ava scratched at her *grande* coffee's cardboard sleeve. The skin under Ava's eyes was dark and agitated, covered in layers of makeup that didn't quite seem to cover it all. Her hair was in a messy bun, and her sweatshirt read *'Namaste in bed.'* Midday sun poured through the floor-to-ceiling windows of the cafe. Clean tables and wooden chairs speckled the lounge. The scent of watered-down bleach commingled with the intoxicating aroma of coffee, giving the place a sanitized but cozy feel.

Madison sat across from her, trying her best to stifle laughter, blonde curls bouncing against her cleavage-baring low-cut sweater. "Oh my God. Only you, Ava. Only *you* could get a black eye on a date."

"Shut up, Madison. It was embarrassing *enough*. Don't pile it on, please."

"I'm sorry." Madison raised her hands defensively and let them fall back to her cup. "Well, third date, at least you got laid. So, how was it? I want *all* the deets. If I feel like you're holding back, I swear to God—"

"I didn't get *laid*."

Madison nearly choked on her coffee. Clearing her throat with a few weak coughs, her mouth fell agape. "You're fuckin' *kidding*, right? The dude's such a slut. Like a *notorious* man-whore!"

Ava shrugged. All the noise from the patrons around them seemed to stop for a moment. "*Thanks* for *that*."

Madison whispered, over-correcting her loud outburst. "I'm serious. He's slept with a *lot* of my friends."

"Yeah. Sure. *Right*." Ava rolled her eyes. "Who? We both know I'm your only friend."

Madison clutched her hand to her hiked breasts. "I have… *lots*… of friends besides you."

"Like who?" Ava smirked.

"Like…" she thought for a moment, "*Trish*."

"Oh, please! Trish is a gossip."

"Well, she's still my *friend*."

"No, she's your drama spigot. You crank the wheel, and that shit pours outta her like a faucet. You think *she'd* have come to bail you outta jail back in the day when you got caught stealing that standee from Blockbuster?"

"First of all, I was like *nineteen* when that happened."

"Yeah. No longer a minor. I had to come get you out of big-boy jail."

"*Second*, okay, Brad Pitt was fuckin' dreamy. What can I say? I'm a slut for androgynous vampires in pirate garb! Plus," Madison scrunched her eyebrows together humorously, "is that really how we are quantifying what counts as a real friend? Someone who can provide bail?"

"I mean, it's a pretty good metric."

Madison waved her hands in front of her. "Stop using words like *metric*. That's why you don't get *laid*. Dudes don't like women who show off how smart they are like that."

"Oh my God, you just used the word *quantified*."

"Do as I *say*, not as I *do*."

"I'm *not* gonna act like a bimbo just to appease men."

"Fine." Madison crossed her arms. "But I have it on good authority—"

"You mean *Trish-the-Mouth* told you."

"*Shhhhh!* Do you wanna hear this or not?"

Ava mirrored Madison, crossing her arms, too, with an expression that said *get on with it.*

"*He gets around.* He's like a genuine *ho.*"

Ava felt her levels of frustration rise. "If he's such a *ho*, why didn't he even *kiss* me at the end of the date last night?"

Silence filled the air between them.

Madison was rendered speechless…

For *once*.

"You didn't even get a *kiss*?" she crowed loudly. This time, her voice attracted the attention of an irritated nearby patron. Her head whipped toward him. "Buzz off, creep, this is a private conversation."

Ava slunk down in her seat, looked at the man apologetically, and mouthed *'I'm sorry.'*

"Don't make me feel even worse, Madison." Ava shoved the palms of her hands to her face. "I… I don't get it! We were having fun. I was getting all the signs."

Madison leaned back and shrugged. "Maybe it was the blood. Nobody wants to kiss a scabby mess."

"Could be." Ava bobbled her head, eyes still cast to the table between them. "I'm goin' out with him again tomorrow, so we will see."

"Well… that's a good sign!"

"Yeah, I dunno. I really like him. I'm not sure he's attracted to me."

"Oh, come on." Madison set her cup back down. "Seriously, look at you! When you're not all busted up lookin' like you've been chasin' parked cars, you're a *bombshell*. I'd *seen* the caliber of guys you've been able to pull over the years. And oddly enough, you married the ugliest one. Trust me, you're finally battin' in the right *league* now."

"Dan wasn't… *ugly*."

"Yes, he was. Guy had a face like someone lit it on fire and put it out with a shovel."

"No, he didn't."

"He had a face you sit on just so you don't have to *look* at it."

"Good *God*, Maddy!"

"*What*, Harla?" Madison chuckled. "He was a cheatin' prick. Fuck him."

Ava thought back to the affair, ashamed at how many signs and red flags she'd missed. Ava shook the thought away and snickered. "You are such a *dick*, you know that?"

"Hey, you *are* what you *eat*." Madison pretended to wipe the corners of her mouth.

"This is nuts. I've never had to *convince* a man to kiss me before."

"It'll be worth the wait when he does, I'm sure. Shit'll probably make your toes curl."

"Yeah, maybe."

"What if I told you that I heard from a *very* trusted source—"

"*Trish*."

" — That he has a big dick?" Madison continued, talking over her.

Ava slowly sat up, rolling her shoulders back into a more confident posture. "How… uh… how big we talkin'?"

"My source—"

"*Trish.*"

"—Said her sister's friend calls him *Will the Impaler.*"

Ava sat silent for a moment and nodded. "I mean, it can't hurt to wait a little longer. You know, just see how things go."

15

Sprawled out on her couch with Kuda stretched along her lap, Ava lounged in pajama pants and a lace-edged camisole as the early evening loomed outside, cold and oppressive. Victor Fleming's *Joan of Arc* played over the large screen, her second time watching it in all of its monochrome glory.

Her cell phone dinged on the coffee table, its screen lighting up brighter than the television. Careful not to wake Kuda, she snatched it up.

It was a text from Will.

WILL: How do women instinctively know how to braid hair?

AVA: It's in our DNA. Why? Are you thinking about trying to braid yours? It's a little too short for that.

WILL: Very funny.

WILL: No. I'm watching a tutorial on it right now online, and it looks like some sort of sorcery. Starla has a crush on a boy in her class, and she keeps asking me to do her hair in one to impress him or something. Have any tips for me?

AVA: Hard to explain. I can't really describe the process well over the phone. It's something you have to practice firsthand.

WILL: Dang.
AVA: You could come over, and I could show you if you want.

WILL: I thought you'd never ask.

WILL: There's just one thing...

**WILL: Starla's on a field
trip. Her class is doing a
whole Fort Caspar butter-
churning their own butter
thing.**

AVA: Oh.

Ava thought hard, scanning her mind to
make up an excuse to still invite him over. Her
heart thundered at the thought of being alone
with him tonight.

**AVA: I still have my
Daenerys Targaryen wig
from a costume party we
had at work last Halloween.
If you wanted to come over,
I could teach you on that.**

Ava's smile fell when the responses ceased.
Fuck. I was too forward. I look desperate now.
Suddenly, three bubbles popped up on the screen,
followed by a message moments later.

**WILL: Sorry. I fainted at
the thought of you dressed
as the Mother of Dragons**

and had to be resuscitated. I'm back now. EMTs said that was a close call. Got a nasty concussion, but they said I'll live.

AVA: Thank God.

WILL: Yes. I think it would be in my daughter's best interest if you taught me that critical skill.

WILL: Like... right away.

WILL: Sooner, the better. Plus, you can keep me awake. The medics said I am not supposed to go to sleep for a while.

AVA: Of course. Due to the concussion.

WILL: Due to the concussion, yes.

AVA: So this is a win-win for you.

WILL: Very much so, yes.

AVA: You still have the address?

WILL: Yes, I do.

AVA: The door is unlocked. Come on in when you get here.

WILL: I'm on my way. This braid thing feels very life or death, and I can't handle that kind of pressure. I'm just a maid!

Ava smiled at her phone and then bit her lip, ignoring the television in front of her. She pet Kuda's head until his warm chocolate eyes slid open. He did a lazy stretch, got up, and trotted to the kitchen.

Ava lifted her arm and smelled herself. She recoiled. A quick shower and shave of the armpits were definitely in order. Darting to the bathroom, she turned on the shower water and stripped naked. Sprinting to the bedroom, she whipped open her dresser drawers, frantically grabbed a matching bra and underwear set, and scurried back to the bathroom. She hurled the clothes on the floor and stepped into the shower, her muscles immediately relaxing with the downpour of hot water. She lathered her hair with a liberal amount of sudsy shampoo, sprayed shave gel on her legs and armpits, and started shaving in a flurry of wet movement.

The sound of her front door opening and closing made her smile.

Fuck, he got there quick.

She shouted loudly past the shower curtain. "I'll be out in a minute!"

She grinned wide like a Cheshire cat.

Fuck it.

"That is… unless you feel like joining me."

"You talked me into it," a man's muffled voice said.

She knew the voice. It was familiar.

But it wasn't Will's…

Her eyes bulged, and a dollop of shampoo ran into them. She furiously swiped away, smearing eye makeup across her face.

The sound of shoes and jeans hitting the floor was followed by the high tone of the shower rings as the curtain slid open.

That was when the source of the voice finally registered in her flustered brain.

Dan, the cheater.

Dan, the *liar*.

Dan, the piece of human garbage who knocked up his secretary and left the piss-covered stick in the kitchen trash for her to find.

Ava screamed. Dan tumbled back, tripping out of the shower and nearly falling onto the cold tile floor, catching himself on the cluttered counter just in time.

Ava darted out of the shower, water still running, and snatched a towel from the rack with a flailing hand. Suds burned her eyes, making her ex-husband difficult to see as she skidded through the hall on wet feet and bolted for her bedroom.

Dan rapped on the locked door a moment later. "Ava, *honey…* we need to talk."

The pause in his speech was a tell that Ava knew all too well from years of dinner parties, work functions, and cookouts with the man: Dan was drunk.

She scrambled for underwear and a bra from her dresser and hurriedly put them on, shampoo stinging her eyes as she bent down to yank up her panties. "*Daaaaaaan!* You were *naked* in my *shower*! Why are you in *my* house?!" She stressed the word 'my,' which was a subtle dig at her getting to keep the place after the split by the judge's order. "We're divorced, *remember*?"

"Please come out... so we can talk."

Yep, definitely drunk. She could almost smell the pickling of his liver through the wood of the door.

"No, Daniel. Get your clothes and go home! You know, your *new* home, with your fiancee and *baby*!" Bitterness was prominent in her indignant tone. She tossed on a baggy t-shirt and pajama shorts from the hamper, the first thing she could get her hands on.

"Please, just... come out... and talk to me."

Ava unlocked the door and yanked it open, eyes smeared with mascara and eyeliner, white, bubbling foam dripping down the sides of her face and onto her chin like a makeshift Santa beard. "What?! What the *hell* do you want?"

Dan's hazel eyes looked back at her. Black bags hung beneath them. His typically-shaven face was coated in something of a 10 o'clock shadow. He looked like he hadn't slept in a *week*. "Ava... I'm fucking miserable. I made... a mistake. I want our life back."

Ava softened a little. "*What*?"

"If I go... put my clothes back on... will you listen to what I have to say?"

It was only then that Ava looked down and realized Dan was naked except for wet calf-high socks and his smartwatch. He cupped his privates in both hands and slouched.

"If it makes you go away faster, then fine."

With a quick nod of understanding, Dan scurried back to the bathroom and grabbed his clothes, talking through the open door. "I really wanted kids, Ava. I really thought I'd really be missing out if I didn't have one."

"I said we could adopt," she yelled back.

"It's not the same. I wanted one of my *own*." His voice was muffled as he pulled his shirt over his head, wearing it backward and inside out now. "Don't get me wrong… I care about Nancy. I really do. I just think… we'd be better off raising Hunter as friends." He bobbled, nearly toppling over in his stupor. He caught himself on the doorknob just in time.

"So split up and share custody like normal adults. What does any of this have to do with you climbing into your ex-wife's fucking shower?!"

"I don't think… I'm cut out to be a Dad." Dan followed her out to the living room, using the walls to right himself, stopping just two feet shy of Ava. Her arms were crossed, and a scowl was plastered across her shampoo-streaked face. "I think… we had it right all along. I was just… too blind to see it. But I see things *clearly* now."

Dan's bloodshot eyes were wild with desperation. Fury bubbled in Ava. *The man had some balls.*

"You look exhausted. You need some rest."

"The kid… he cries… all the time!"

"That's part of *having a kid*, Daniel. That's what you signed up for."

"I know. Look," he said frantically, grabbing Ava's hand, "I know."

Ava jerked her hand away from him and growled, "*You did this to yourself. All of it, Dan!* You got another woman knocked up. And I'm supposed to just *shrug that off*? I can't have *kids*! Do you *know* how fucking hurtful that is to do to someone? You tossed me aside like I was useless garbage. You put your own needs first. You always have!" Ava felt the last of her restraint crumble beneath the strain of her words.

"You were gone all of the time for your *job*!" He yelled. "I was lonely! I handled it the wrong way. I'm sorry, Ava, but you can't let one stupid decision ruin twelve years of being together."

"No, *you* did."

"We can go back to the way things were. We were so… happy."

"I wasn't happy! I was *comfortable*. There's a difference. Clearly, you were missing something I couldn't give you."

"You were never around!" He bobbed his head. "Although, I'm sorry. I heard you lost your job."

Ava was appalled. "From *who*?"

"It's a small town, Ava. Word gets around."

"So? I lost my *job*, not my *mind*. You need to leave!" Ava sneered and jabbed her finger towards the door.

"I'm not going anywhere, Ava," Dan continued, grabbing her arms and drawing her closer. "You love me. I know you do."

"I do not *need* this right now!" Ava groaned and tried to pull away. His grip tightened, and he tugged her back. "I *loved* you. Past tense, Dan. Now let me go! I am not going to ask you again!"

"I'm sorry! How many different ways do I need to say it? Do you want me to scream it from the roof? Take out a fucking *billboard*? I'm sorry! I was an idiot!"

"You were a terrible husband. You never know what you actually want. You always think you *need* what you can't *have*."

"Just give me a chance!" He yanked her close and forced his thin lips against hers.

It was like kissing two chapped worms.

The front door opened. Will waltzed in with a paddle brush in his hand, smiling as if he were about to say something clever. But he froze in the doorway, stunned by the image of Dan kissing Ava right in front of him. Will gritted his jaw and turned to leave.

Ava pulled away from Dan, attempting to wrench herself from his arms. "Wait, Will! It's not what you think! He wasn't invited! He won't leave! Please… help me get him out of here!"

Her words rang out in Will's ears over the pounding of his pulse. He whipped around and looked at the hold Dan had on her arms.

"What's going on? Is this asshole *hurting* you?" The look in his eyes said that a singular nod of her head would make him launch on the male stranger and pound his fist until the guy was missing teeth.

"He's fucking *leaving*." Ava whipped her arms away from Dan. "*Aren't* you?"

"Who the fuck is *this*? Got yourself a new little boy-toy, Ave?" Daniel snarled.

Kuda erupted in a symphony of vicious barks from the entrance to the nearby kitchen.

"I'm her *boyfriend*, you scumbag."

Despite the soap bubbling against her scalp and the agitation from the scene Dan was causing, Ava fought the urge to smile. Even though Will said it to intimidate the man, something about the sound of it…

Felt *right*.

"Ava? Should *I* leave? Or should *he*?"

"Him!" Ava pointed to Dan like she was a tattling teenager, heart pounding. "Will, I *swear* to you, I did not invite him over. He's drunk and just… came in while I was in the shower." She pressed her wrist to her forehead for a second to put pressure on her forming headache. Shampoo foam transferred. She grimaced and wiped it on her clothes. "This is Dan. My *ex*-husband," she said, stressing the 'ex' loudly.

Will rolled his shoulders back and took another step in. "Look, *Dan*, if you would like to keep all your bones unbroken and your teeth in your gums, you need to leave. *Now*."

"You're sleep-deprived. You aren't thinking straight. Just go home!" Ava used both hands to push Dan toward Will. Again, Kuda's bark rang out.

"Give me another chance!" Dan yanked Ava toward him by her shirt and kissed her.

Will's fist crashed into Dan's jaw, dropping him to the floor. Ava gasped, covered her face, and leaped backward. Kuda raced to Daniel's pant leg and tore at the hem of his jeans, shredding fabric.

"Kuda, stop!" Ava pulled at her dog's collar until he backed up.

Will stood over Dan with readied fists. "The lady asked you to leave."

"That's assault, fuckface." Dan looked at Ava. "You're just gonna let him hit me?! Aren't you gonna *do* anything?"

Will snatched Dan by the inside-out shirt and thrust him onto his feet. "Let's go, Romeo."

Ava and Kuda watched from the kitchen doorway as Will tossed Dan out into the snow-covered yard.

Will grabbed the door handle. "You ever think about touching her again I'll break every single one of your fucking fingers."

Dan nodded, sobering in the frozen pile of fluff.

Will slammed the door and locked it.

Ava stepped into the living room, tears welling in her eyes. "I'm sorry, Will. He just showed up. I haven't seen him in months! I thought he was *you*. He just climbed into the shower with me!"

She wiped a dripping dollop of sudsy water from her brow before it could sting her eyes further.

Will clenched his teeth. "Did he hurt you?"

"No, he just scared me."

"Okay. Good." Will exhaled long and slow, looking up at Ava. "Go ahead and finish your shower. I'll make sure he doesn't come back."

***

A shared pint of Neapolitan ice cream and two classic feature films later, Ava found herself on the couch, wrapped in Will's comforting embrace, her head relaxed on his shoulder, dangling, once again, on the precipice of sleep.

As the credits rolled, Will chanced a glance down at Ava and smiled. She grabbed the remote and clicked off the television. Without a word, she wiggled from his embrace and extended her hand to him.

Barely able to see, Will tilted his head curiously and finally took it.

"Will you stay with me tonight? I feel a little freaked out still."

Though it seemed understandable, Will had no idea how he would be able to do so and keep his hands to himself. "I… don't know."

"Look, Will, I completely respect that you don't want to do more. We could just… *sleep*. I just feel vulnerable. He broke into my *house*."

"It's not that I don't want to do more…"

"You don't need to explain. You're allowed to do things in your own time and feel how you feel. You can't rush a good thing."

He could feel her smile through the darkness, sense it in her voice.

"I just feel like he's going to barge back in here at any minute."

"Yeah, I don't have any clients until eleven tomorrow." His watch lit up in the black void and gently lit his face before returning to his side. "I can stay."

"Thank you."

Ava reached for his hand. When she found it in the darkness, she led him to the bedroom. Once there, Will grinned, his stunning smile faintly visible in the room streaked with slivers of white through the blinds. The light played off the features of her face, and he wished he could take a photograph of her, capturing the moment forever. She was a goddess bathed in moonlight.

He grinned, leaning against the doorway to mentally soak her in like a sponge. "You are so damned beautiful."

Kuda padded in and curled up on the large dog bed in the corner. Ava smiled, whipped back the covers of the bed, and patted the Egyptian cotton sheets. "I promise I won't bite."

"I usually don't sleep in anything but boxers."

"*Hallelujah*," Ava howled.

Will snickered, tugged off his shirt, and set it on the dresser. His pants followed. He climbed beneath the covers, and Ava wriggled backward, nestling against his muscular chest. A weighty arm wrapped around her, pulling her close.

"Do you snore?" he asked quietly.

"Almost never. I promise, if I snore, you can just make me go sleep in Kuda's bed."

He laughed and brushed a lock of hair from the side of her face, trailing his fingers delicately along her scalp. "I would never do that to any woman."

"You're a gem."

"Even if you snore, I'm sure it'd be more cute than anything."

Ava relaxed into his cuddle, tucking her damp head beneath his chin. The apricot and lemongrass conditioner left her air smelling like an orchard he blissfully wanted to escape to and live forever.

"Thank you for this," Ava cooed sweetly.

"Any time I get to hold you, it is my pleasure." He kissed the top of her head and wrapped his arms around her tighter. "Goodnight, Ava."

16

"So, do you like her?" Starla asked, shoveling an awkward forkful of spaghetti into her mouth.

"You're too young for me to be talking about this kind of stuff with," Will muttered, swirling more spaghetti around his fork.

"I'm six years old. That's practically an adult."

Will snorted. "Well then. Since you're an *adult*, we should discuss you paying rent."

"You're ignoring my question. I wanna know! Is she nice?"

"She's very nice."

"Is she pretty?"

Will swallowed another bite. "She's stunning."

"What does that mean? She's ugly?"

"No. It means she's *beyond* pretty. She's beautiful."

"*Oh.*" Starla stuffed more spaghetti into her mouth, dropping some down her pink shimmery shirt. "*Do 'ou fink she'd wike me?*" Long noodles tumbled from her young mouth onto the table.

"Stop talking with your mouth full. We talked about that, hun."

"Sorry." She mumbled through the starch and sauce. She swallowed. "When do I get to meet her?"

"Sweetheart, I can't introduce you until I know she's going to be around a while. You don't deserve to get attached to people who may not stick around."

"Okay." Her little voice was tinged with sadness.

"Is that alright?"

She shrugged her shoulders and thought for a moment. She grabbed another forkful of food, slurping it and smearing the tomato sauce across the lower half of her face. "It would be nice to have another girl around so we can do stuff like painting our nails and doing our hair, and we can have parties with my stuffed animals."

"But Star, you and I can do all of that together."

"You'll let me paint your fingernails?"

Will tilted his head as if to say, *'Really?'*

Her deep, blue eyes widened, sad like a begging puppy.

Will shook his head and looked down. Gremlin sat beside his chair, staring up at him with the same expression. "Oh, now I am getting ganged up on? The both of you are working together? I see how it is."

After a long silence, he spoke. "Yes, you can paint my nails."

Starla gasped with joy.

"But… daddy gets to take it off before work, okay?"

"I'm gonna go get my nail polishes!" Starla scurried from the table.

Will shouted, "*Starla Mae Jessup.*"

She froze in place and pivoted on the balls of her socked feet. "Yesssss?"

"Spaghetti first. Nails later," he grumbled.

She trudged back to the table, trying to hide her grin.

"…And nothing with *glitter.*"

17

Darcy Higgins liked her home in pristine condition. Her walls were gleaming white, from the kitchen cabinets to the glossy stone flooring.

Every time Will walked in, it felt like he was looking at a surgeon's light or peering straight at Heaven. The starkness of it all often left him with a headache. Plus, she was a flirt, to say the least. The juxtaposition of her dirty mind with her overly sterile environment made his head spin.

Darcy was an attractive thirty-five-year-old. Her husband was allegedly an older, highly sought-after neurosurgeon, though Will had never met him. Darcy's husband's trips to medical conventions often left the lonely woman at home… with no children, hobbies, or close friendships to occupy her time.

That's where Will came into play.

Today, he was dressed in a trench coat and a hat with little else, like some male stripper version of Dick Tracy. Though the uniforms were listed on his website, this one was a special request, an option with an exorbitant fee that some women were more than happy to pay. In his arms, he held a handled bucket full of potting soil, a prop unsurprisingly hard to find in the midst of a harsh Wyoming winter.

Darcy was swathed in a pink nightgown beneath a sheer, feather-lined robe, sleek caramel hair framing her face. "Let me see it."

Will stripped off his jacket, exposing a bare body, save for a pair of black Balenciaga boxer briefs that left almost nothing to the imagination. He looked like an underwear model in little more than a pair of combat boots.

"Oh, I love them! I'm so glad they were the right size. Sometimes, these fashion brands run a little small."

Will nodded as he stretched, loosening up tight muscles. "They fit perfectly. Weirdly enough, I've never had a more comfortable pair of underwear in my life."

"You're more than welcome," she cooed. "For five hundred bucks, they better handle your nuts like an angel's palm."

Will shook his head and laughed as he breezed past her to the kitchen. He stuck the bucket in the sink and turned the faucet on. After filling it a third of the way up, he mashed the black contents with his hands, lifted the bucket back out, and poured the mud slop all over the floor. As Darcy squealed with joy, stepping back to avoid the dark splatter, Will fought the urge to grimace at how strange he felt her fetish was. He plopped the bucket back in the sink and squished his boots through the mud, doing a model walk down her hallway into the white marble den and back again, tracking black bootprints all throughout the area.

Darcy panted with excitement, aroused. "Yesssssss!"

"Why don't you take a seat." He pulled out a chair at the kitchen's bar and motioned to it. "From right here, you should be able to enjoy the whole show."

He knew what he was doing. If he could get her to sit, she'd be less likely to try to be frisky and break the no-touch rule, as she had several times before.

She nodded and took a seat. Her eyes were wide, bouncing between his face, chest, the bulge in his underwear, the mud on the floor, and back again.

"I'm going to get the mop. I'll just be a moment."

"Hurry back." She waggled her fingers at him.

Again, he tracked a path of mud across the stone floor out into the garage. Flicking the high-powered LED lights on, the glare from the vehicles made him squint. He glanced past the Audi, Mercedes, and Bugatti to the far corner beyond. He spotted a red bucket and several vehicle sponges, among other detailing items. He traipsed across the epoxy floor, grabbed what he needed, and left the heated garage.

Once back in the kitchen, he filled the water reservoir, grabbed a sponge, got down on his hands and knees, and wiped at the edges of the huge mess, trying his best to angle in a way that would showcase the expensive underwear she'd ordered him.

***

Nearly done sponging and mopping the mess, Will heard the front door unlock and open. A man in his sixties stared at Will — and then Will's *underwear* — with a look of utter shock. Will was afraid the old man was going to have a heart attack on the spot.

"What the hell is going on here?"

"Honey!" There was a note of fear blended with anxiety in Darcy's voice despite trying to sound chipper. "You're home… *early*."

"Good afternoon, sir." Will dropped the sponge and stood, dangling his hands in front of his crotch. "You are Mr. Higgins, I presume."

Silence.

Will cleared his throat. "My name is Will Jessup. I'm just here to clean."

"Oh, I'm *sure*," the man scoffed.

"It's true, Hank. He's just here to clean."

"In his fucking underwear, Darcy? How stupid do you think I am?!"

"Mr. Higgins, I promise you, I am just here to clean. I can grab you one of my cards if you'd like." He gestured to the khaki trench coat hanging on the rack beside the older man.

"He doesn't sleep with clients, Hank. He just *cleans*." Darcy stared into Hank's eyes.

"What are you, some kind of sex worker? Are you two *fucking* when I go out of town?"

Will raised his hands defensively. "No, sir. I just clean. That's all. Nothing untoward."

"Get out of my fucking house!" Hank spat, pointing at the front door.

Will scrambled to put on his boots and rushed out in nothing but shoes and underwear, laces still untied. The cold hit him like an icy train crashing into his bare skin. The door slammed shut behind him.

Will turned around, realizing he had left his trench coat inside. The truck keys were still in his coat pocket.

Fuck, fuck, fuck!

He scurried back up the steps, hesitating to knock despite the freezing temps. Inside, he heard Hank screaming at the top of his lungs.

Will tried the knob, and the door quietly opened. He stepped inside and snatched his coat, tipping the rack over onto the floor. Will swiped at it, but it was too far out of reach.

"Don't do anything stupid, Hank! He just did what I paid him to do," She wailed.

Mr. Higgins stormed toward Will.

"I'll fucking kill you, you son of a bitch!"

Will darted out the door, slipping on the ice and splaying hard across the stoop. Will looked up just as a fist plummeted toward his face. He rolled and heard bones crack hard against the stone beneath him.

Hank screamed, gripping his busted fist in pain.

Will clambered to his booted feet and stepped back out of Hank's reach. "Jesus, are you *alright*?"

"Do I fuckin' *look* alright? I think I just fractured my goddamned metacarpal!" Mr. Higgins shouted, slinking down onto the cold stone floor, clutching his trembling hand.

Will stepped down onto the snowy lawn, packed two handfuls together in his hands like a snowball, and returned to Hank's side. "Here. Put some ice on it.."

Mr. Higgins spiked the snowy lump onto the stone steps with his uninjured hand like a volleyball, flashing Will a devastatingly loathsome gaze. "Get the fuck out of here!"

Will held his hands up and backed away slowly. From the doorway, Darcy tossed him his trench coat with an apologetic stare.

Will put it on and trudged back to his truck, cinching it shut. He hopped in and slammed the door behind him. Hank yowled like a cat in heat as Darcy tried to wrap her arms around him. He shrugged her off and growled something Will couldn't make out.

Mrs. Higgins looked up at Will and waved goodbye.

Will knew it was *for good.*

New rule, he thought to himself as he pulled away, *always keep a spare set of keys in the glove box…*

18

"So why are we waiting outside in the middle of January?" Ava's words came out in puffy billows of steam as the icy air nipped at her lungs. Despite the mid-afternoon sunshine, the unforgiving cold lingered.

"You'll see soon enough. If we wait inside, it would spoil the surprise. They announce it over the speakers once every few minutes. It's worth the cold, I promise. That's why I wanted you to dress warm."

"I did," she added, gesturing to her puffy coat, boots, beanie and gloves. "None of it does diddly-squat for this Wyoming *wind,* though." Her teeth chattered violently.

Will chuckled, wrapping a strong arm around her. "Is that better?"

"Not really," she answered honestly with a shrug.

"Here." He positioned himself between her and the wind, unzipped his coat, and held it open for her. "*Come.*"

Ava grinned and obliged, burrowing beneath his coat like a down-clad tick. Her face rested against his chest, and he closed his coat around the both of them.

"Better?" he asked as the shivering against him slowly subsided.

"*Much.*"

Will smiled, resting his chin against the top of her head. "I never realized how short you were until right now."

"These boots don't have heels," Ava's muffled voice muttered.

Horses clomped in the distance as Ava basked in Will's radiant warmth like a lizard on a hot rock.

Will finally spoke, vibrating her face with his low voice. "Your carriage awaits, my lady."

"Carriage?!" Ava echoed, prying herself from Will's chest to see two horses approaching with a decorative wooden cart, every edge laced with faux flowers in various colors.

"Oh my God! I know where we're going!"

"No, you don't," Will said incredulously.

"Yes, I do! There's only one reason for a cart in Jackson Hole. The National Elk Refuge!"

Will was stunned that she guessed the surprise. "Ever been?"

"No!" She beamed. "I've always wanted to see it, though! Just never made the time."

"Well," Will walked to the carriage and extended a hand to her, "Ladies first!"

Ava's cheeks were red with excitement and cold as she climbed aboard. Will followed. As they took their seats, the cart took off.

"I can't believe you did this!"

"I actually bought all the seats so we could have the carriage to ourselves."

"Aww!"

"Thought it would be a little more romantic that way." Will shrugged with a smile.

Ava scooted closer to him, and he wrapped his arm around her, pulling her in until their legs touched each other.

"Howdy folks!" hollered the coachman. His gravelly voice was that of a pack-a-day smoker. "It's a *cold* one today. We have blankets on the other side if you want to bundle up together. That wind is givin' you a real *Wyomin' welcome*."

Ava pulled her beanie down over her rowdy, wind-blown hair and smiled brightly.

"You folks from around here?" The man asked over his shoulder.

Will spoke up over the wind. "We both live here. Just thought it would be a fun experience. This is her first time."

"You've been before?" Ava asked, scooting so close that the heat from his breath warmed her ear.

"Yeah. But it's always a treat."

Hopping off the paved road onto a snowy path, the cart rumbled toward a massive herd of elk. Ava watched in wonder, mouth open in amazement at the sheer amount of four-legged creatures strewn throughout the field beyond.

The elk barely stirred at the sight of the cart as it dipped and swayed with the uneven ground. The wagon approached a large herd, passing by a full cart of passengers snapping photos and excitedly chatting like two ships on the open seas. The drivers nodded to one another.

As Will and Ava's carriage hobbled closer, the elk turned their head to look at them. White puffs of smoke tumbled from their nostrils as they cautiously watched the cart rumble by. The majority of the animals remained unbothered, bedded down in the melting snow, hides twitching with the breeze.

"Holy cow, they are *massive!*" Ava gaped over the side of the cart as the living mounds of muscle stood still and stoic beside them. In the distance, cows butted heads, mewling as they battled. A beastly elk with massive antlers lay down amid a cluster of females.

Settling into his role, the coachman spoke over the wind. "The females, or cows, are the ones without antlers. A group of them together is called *a harem*. Bull elks, like those two back there, can be challenged for the possession of their harem at any time. The males clash antlers, and if one antler gets mangled or busted, they lose their appeal and become less desirable to the females."

Ava watched two cows butt heads in the distance.

"What about them? Those are females, right? Why are they butting heads?"

"For a higher spot in the harem. They bicker over men just like women do." The coachman laughed, tickled by his own comment.

Ava stared out at the sporadic puffs of white smoke. Countless eyes stared back at them as though *they* were the creatures really on display.

"They're *gorgeous*," Ava cooed, turning in her seat to watch the elk. The carriage got so close to some that Ava could see the burnt-orange hue of their irises.

Will spread his arms across the top of the cart behind them and took in the incredible view of the snow-dusted mountain range and colorful, wide-open Wyoming sky. Rolling hills dipped down to the large valley that hundreds of elk called home. Pristine fields of undisturbed white snow surrounded them in nearly every direction.

"It's incredible that they know this place is safe," Ava mused. "These are massive beasts that we can't talk to or communicate, and they have learned to trust people and allow the cart to pass."

Will smiled, overjoyed at the childlike wonder on Ava's face. She looked like she was watching a magic act.

The coachmen laughed. "These elk are here because they know this is a refuge. Hunters scare them to this place, or they come in search of food. Don't touch their calves, keep a wide berth, and you'll be fine."

Will chuckled. "They're just like us. All they want is salt, safety, and sex."

"*Salt*?" Ava asked, trying to keep her mind off of the latter. *Or lack thereof...*

The coachman hacked and cleared his throat. "Ever heard of the saying *'antlers still in velvet'*?"

Ava nodded, studying the man as if she would be tested on the subject.

"Well, those antlers take a lot of minerals to grow. The elk are attracted to salt lick stands and seek a variety of nutrients to regrow their antlers after they fall off. The 'velvet' is actually thousands of tiny blood vessels. They eventually die off and itch, so the elk rub 'em against tree bark and branches to get 'em off."

"*Cool*." Ava stared at one of the thick sets of antlers and wondered how many minerals it must've taken to grow a set of antlers that massive.

"Another little-known fact: their teeth are valuable. Besides being hunted for their racks and meat, certain elk teeth are made of *ivory* and are used to make jewelry."

"I tried to get into hunting," Will admitted, "but something about their *eyes*… I could never pull the trigger. They're not dumb animals. They have their own language, their own customs. I respect the hell out of hunting, but elk… I just can't do it."

Ava nestled into the crook of Will's arm and smiled contentedly.

Will and Ava enjoyed the rest of the ride in silence, soaking in the breathtaking view of a wilderness that stretched miles ahead.

19

As Will walked her back to her car, Ava jangled her keys in her hand and leaned against the driver's side door. "Thank you for this. It was fascinating. And thank you for making sure we had the cart to ourselves. That's one of the sweetest things anyone has done for me in a looooong time."

"I'm just glad we could spend some time together." He pressed his hand to the SUV and leaned in. Ava felt her hands go clammy. *But she was ready for this.*

Ready for *him*.

She looked at his lips, slightly wind-burned from the blistering cold but still utterly delectable. He stared at her for a moment.

This was it.

"Drive safe, okay?"

He pushed away from the car and turned to leave.

"Wh-what the *hell*?" Ava uttered aloud, flabbergasted.

Will turned around and chuckled. "What?"

"What do you mean, *what*? This is like our fourth date, and I haven't gotten so much as a kiss from you. Do you not find me attractive?"

"Why would you even *think* that?"

"Because you haven't tried to kiss me. You haven't put the moves on me at all. From what I've heard," her eyes bulged, "I dunno. I just... thought this would go differently."

Will's expression turned serious, and he shoved his hands into his pockets. "Whatever you've heard from the women around here... that is who I *used* to be. I'm trying very hard *not* to be that guy anymore. I want something different. Something deep. Something real. And I can't figure out what that is if I'm just focusing on getting in someone's pants." He stepped closer. "Look, I'm no prude. It's not like I'm saving myself for marriage or anything. But, you... I don't know. You seem... special."

His cobalt eyes met hers, and she felt her knees buckle. She leaned against her Denali to save her from falling.

"I do?"

"Yes!" he said with a laugh into the air. "Ava, I'm trying to take this slow and get to know you because... I don't want this to be just some fling. I think you're fucking amazing. And I'm not here to just play games or add to my body count. I… I want a wife. I want real love, Ava."

Silence filled the frozen air between them.

"I enjoy spending time with you, Ava. You're fun and bubbly and spontaneous. You're not afraid to take a risk and look like a fool sometimes. You're different than anyone I've ever met, and if I kiss you…"

"If you kiss me… *what*?" Ava asked, feeling her stomach flip as she waited for the answer.

"If I *kiss* you, I swear to God, Ava, with lips like yours, I won't be able to stop."

Ava felt like she couldn't breathe. Her body felt like a furnace suddenly, as if she might look down and see a circle of snow melted down to the grass beneath all around her.

"You are so fucking beautiful. And the fact that you are a teensy bit of a *mess* drives me crazy, in a *good* way. I just… I don't wanna screw this up."

Ava nodded and smiled. "I can respect that."

"Thank you." Will stuffed his hands into his back pockets, spreading the lapels of his jacket open enough for her to glimpse the shirt clinging to his firm chest beneath. Without thinking, she bit her lip.

"So, if not a kiss… then how do we end a date as nice as this? Fist bumps? High-five? Is this a slap-on-the-ass 'good game' situation?"

Will laughed. "We say goodbye, and you text me the next night you're free so I can take you out again."

Ava smirked, blushing. "Goodbye, Will Jessup."

"Goodbye, Ava Quinn." He smiled back and blew her a kiss from across the parking lot.

She caught it and held it close to her heart.

20

Will let the shower rain down on his muscles. The chilled water did nothing to soothe his throbbing hard-on. His mind raced back to the moment Ava had asked him about the kiss. In his fantasy, he lunged, pressing her against her SUV and kissing her with every ounce of passion in his body, hands roaming over the curves of her sweater, feeling her knee slide against his rigid cock as he pressed against her. He'd wanted to pick her up, right then and there, and fuck her in the back seat until the windows fogged into an opaque wall of gray.

He stroked himself, imagining her silken tongue sliding against his before moving his mouth to her breasts, her mouth moaning into his ear as her body shuddered at his touch. His groin swelled to the point of pain at the thought.

He needed her.

Needed to be *with* her.

Needed to be *inside of* her...

He pumped his shaft with an eager hand, aching for relief. He braced against the shower tiles and pictured Ava's lips and tongue sliding down his hardened shaft. He let the shower water blast against his face as the familiar sensation of an impending orgasm built.

His mind flitted to rubbing her pussy through the fabric of her panties. Pulling them to the side and slipping a finger into the wetness beyond. He imagined burying his face between her legs, lapping up every drop of her as she begged for more.

"*Fuck*," he growled quietly into the tile, water caressing his open lips. He came so hard he had to hold the soap dish to keep from collapsing to the tub of the floor, flexing every muscle of his body as each lustful spurt swirled down the drain. A clarity befell him, and his body relaxed to a zen-like level, temporarily sated. It was the fifth time in three days he'd touched himself to the thought of her.

21

Will lay in bed with boxers on, flipping through the social media apps on his phone, listening to Starla's gentle snoring from the next room when his phone chimed, and a text alert popped up at the top of his screen from his best friend, Barrett.

BARRETT: Sup dink? When are we gonna hit the gym? Doc finally cleared me for exercise again.

He stared at it for a moment and set the phone down in his lap. The device chimed again. Another notification lit up the screen: a message from Ava.

AVA: You up?

Will smiled at his phone and quickly responded to her.

WILL: Did you seriously just send me the 'you up' text? Ava... I'm not that kind of girl.

AVA: LOL. I didn't mean it like that. I just couldn't sleep.

AVA: Glad to see I'm not the only one.

Will scrunched his eyebrows in confusion. *What time is it?* He glanced up at the clock on his phone and grimaced. One-twelve A.M.

WILL: Wow. I didn't realize it was this late.

AVA: Want me to let you go? I'm sure you need sleep.

WILL: No, not yet. I actually have a question for you.

AVA: Shoot.

WILL: Did you ever go to your prom?

AVA: Yeah. Both years. Why?

WILL: I never went to any of mine.

Will waited for a moment, flipping back to his social media feed to double-check the date and time on a virtual invitation.

WILL: What are you doing Tuesday night?

AVA: Oh, geez. Let me check my busy calendar.

WILL: Wanna go to prom with me?

AVA: Um... what? I think I'm about fourteen years too late for that.

WILL: My daughter's specialist is hosting a

charity event for children
with diabetes. It's an adult
prom.

WILL: Would you like to
go to prom with me?

Will waited while a text bubble with an
ellipsis popped up and disappeared numerous
times. He could see her struggling with her
decision.

AVA: I'd love to go to
prom with you. :)

WILL: Great! Pick you up
at 7?

AVA: 7 sounds great. I'll
see you then.

AVA: Oh... and Will?

WILL: Yes?

AVA: Don't forget the
corsage.   My   favorite
flowers are pink cherry
blossoms ;)

22

Clad in a powder-blue dress shirt beneath a charcoal jacket and slacks, Will strode through the snow to Ava's front door and knocked. Beyond the etched glass, he could see the sheen of delicate fabric shimmy in his direction. Ava opened the door, revealing her light pink satin gown with a sweetheart neckline and off-the-shoulder sleeves. Her auburn hair was pinned up in a French twist, framed at the sides by a few delicate stray tendrils.

He didn't blink. "Oh… my. I'm pretty sure my heart just stopped."

Ava swatted his shoulder with her rhinestone clutch purse and giggled. "I'm not certified in CPR, so let's hope not. Ready for your first prom?"

Will chuckled. "Yes, I think so. But I believe the high school prom rules still apply. We have to leave room between us for Jesus."

Will held out an arm, and she took it. Ava laughed. "*What?*"

He walked her down the salted walkway toward his pickup truck. "I think it's a stodgy way of saying 'don't grind on each other on the dance floor.'"

"Ah. Well, that's no fun."

"Your corsage is inside, madame. Along with the little pin thingy for my jacket."

"You really got me a corsage?"

"Of course. Cherry blossoms. As requested."

"Where the hell did you find cherry blossoms in Jackson Hole?"

Will opened the passenger door and helped her up into the seat, hands lingering on her hips for a moment too long. "They had to be imported from China."

"Are you *serious*?" Ava's jaw hung open.

"...At least that's what the little tag said when I bought them from the hobby store." Will beamed and handed her the corsage in a see-through plastic container. Fake cherry blossoms were arranged delicately over a wrist strap.

Ava chuckled. "Thank you."

"Of course," Will said. He cupped her face in his warm hands and planted a kiss on her cheek. He could feel the skin beneath his lips heat as she blushed.

"Hey, in case you didn't know, I really like you," he said lowly, trailing the tip of his nose on the soft skin near her ear.

Ava was speechless, wanting to say so much, but her lips wouldn't cooperate. Without another word, he closed the door and jogged to his side.

Inside, he rubbed his palms together for warmth and started the vehicle. "I feel bad for the guys going to this thing."

"Why?" Ava slid the corsage onto her wrist and fondled the matching boutonniere.

"Because," he pulled out onto the street, watching for cars and pedestrians, "I'll be with the most beautiful woman in there, and all they will be able to do is eat their hearts out. *Sad, really.*"

"Those poor bastards." Ava laughed.

During the entire ride across town, Will's smile never left his face.

***

Teal and purple streamers hung from a chandelier overhead. Matching balloons adorned each table as festive centerpieces. White linens and matching chair covers lent some class to the affair. A large buffet lined a side wall. A bar with eager staff occupied the opposite wall. An oversized dance floor in the center of the hall was sparsely peppered with a few brave souls starting the night off with a slow dance.

A deejay stood at a booth in the center remixing nostalgic 90s slow jams.

Will led Ava out to the center of the dance floor. "90s rock. I like it. Think he'd play it if I requested some Nirvana?"

"No." She laughed, trying not to let her hand tremble in his grasp.

"What about Nine Inch Nails?"

"Look at that goober." She nodded toward the deejay. "The way he's dressed, the only nine inch nails he knows about are the ones used after Judas' betrayal."

"Oof. Alright." He thought for a moment. "What about… TLC? Guy looks like he knows a thing or two about chasin' waterfalls, at the very least."

Ava snickered and soaked in her surroundings. "This whole thing is pretty cute, I must say."

"Yeah, it is. Think I got an invite because I donated to their foundation a while back. Pretty sure I'm on their mailing list for life now."

Ava smiled. "Maybe whatever I do next, I can push for a portion of something to go to a charity like this."

"I think *whatever* you do next, they'll be lucky to have you."

"Thanks." She wrapped her arms around his neck, and he did the same with her waist. In time with the music, they swayed.

In that moment, all that existed in the world was them.

Ava slid a hand up his neck, running her fingers through his thick, dirty blonde hair. Will leaned in and pressed his forehead to hers, lips dangerously close to hers, noses rubbing softly.

"What do you want out of life, Will?"

"I want love. I want to share my life with someone. I want something timeless and passionate, like in the movies. The *'I can't breathe without you* kind of love.' I want to be with someone who challenges me and is driven and fun."

"Wow."Ava felt a pang in her chest. *How could she ever be that for him?*

"What about you," he whispered in her ear. His voice was like a rumble of thunder through her body, making the hairs on her arm stand on end.

"I used to think I knew. Watching my parents grow up, I thought I always wanted what they had. I thought loving someone meant cleaning up after them, making them breakfast, bearing their kids… because that's what I saw growing up. Last time I went back to visit my folks, it broke my heart."

"Why?" His thumbs stroked the dimples at the base of her spine through the fabric of her dress.

"Because it wasn't love. It was just comfort. There was no romance. No desire. And looking back, I don't think there ever was. I had always wanted a love like theirs, and yet, they were sort of… miserable. Love is more than obligation. It's more than flowers on Valentine's Day or a dinner out on your anniversary. It's the electric air in your lungs, the pounding of need in your veins, the feeling of being home when you look into someone's eyes."

"I concur." Will stared at her for a moment, drinking in the sight of her before resting his chin gently atop her head.

She inhaled the woodsy scent of his cologne as the familiar words of a slow-paced love song filled the silence around them. She felt the thud of his heart against her cheek and the warmth of his skin. She wished she could bottle the moment and keep it forever.

Everything felt… *right*. As if nothing had suddenly become *something*. When she imagined her future, he was there. She hadn't planned on becoming this attached to anyone ever again after Dan, but here she was, wrapped in the arms of a man she couldn't seem to get enough of.

Will crooked a finger and brought her chin up with it until he was gazing into her eyes. "This is nice."

"Yes, it is." Her hand caressed the back of his head lovingly. Her face warmed with excitement as his face neared hers, lips nearly brushing her own.

"I really want to kiss you right now."

She could feel his whisper against the skin near her awaiting mouth. "I think you should," she whispered back.

Suddenly, music wafted up from his dress slacks.

"Thaaaat's how country boys roll!"

The tune sounded from his back pocket. His face whipped away as he scrambled in a panic to pick up. It was the ringtone for his home's landline, one that wouldn't sound unless something was crucial. "I'm sorry, it's the babysitter. I *have* to take this."

Will plugged one ear and pulled away, walking back to their table.

Ava stood on the dance floor, suddenly abandoned, looking around. She drifted toward the bar, ordered a cocktail, and watched Will across the room. Her eyes drifted to some women at the next table, eyeing Will like a piece of meat.

Moments later, he approached her with a look of concern on his face. "It's Starla. She's sick. Babysitter said her glucose is, like, alarmingly low."

"Oh no! I am so sorry to hear that." Ava frowned. "Go. Don't worry. I'll Uber home or something."

Will clutched his jacket nervously. "Want to come with me?" He tried to smile and failed. "I don't want this night to end, but I also don't—"

"Say no more." She managed a smile. "I'd love to."

23

Will bolted through the front door and headed toward the teenager sitting on the couch. "Where is she. Is she okay, still?"

"She's doing okay. She's in her room." The teen's hair shot out of the sides of a messy braid, braces gleaming beneath paper-thin lips. "She vomited after dinner. She seems to be doing okay right now, but her numbers are high on her meter. I don't know what's going on."

"It's alright, Amy. I'll get it figured out. We can take it from here." He pulled out his wallet and peeled out some crisp twenties for her.

"Thanks, Mr. Jessup. I hope she feels better."

"I appreciate that. Take care, Amy. Drive safe. They say it's gonna get down to zero tonight. Stay alert for black ice on the road, okay?"

"Sure thing, Mr. Jessup."

"Shoot me a text when you make it home, too, just so I know you didn't end up in a ditch or something, alright?"

Amy nodded and looked at Ava. Ava could swear she saw a flicker of jealousy in the girl's eyes. Amy nodded and made her way out the front door with a wave.

The second the door clicked shut, Will strode down the hallway and rapped on Starla's door once before opening it. The pink room was lit up by a rotating night light plastering garish horse silhouettes on nearly every inch of her wall.

"Hey, Sweet Pea. How you feelin'?"

Starla laid on her side, clutching Gremlin to her chest. The pup's tail *whapped* the bedding at the sight of Will.

"I don't feel so good." Starla's voice was small and meek.

"What happened? You were fine when I left."

Starla shrugged pitifully.

Will sat down beside Gremlin. The dog lovingly licked at his hand as he reached over to feel her head. "You feel a little warm. Lemme check your pump and see where your levels are at, okay?"

"Okay." She grumbled and handed the monitoring device over.

Will looked down at the device, clicking buttons on the interface, and then glanced back at the doorway where Ava timidly lurked in the shadows of the hall. "Starla, this is my friend. Ava."

Will waved Ava inside the room.

Cautiously, she entered, bathed in glowing horse cutouts. "Hi, Starla. I'm sorry you aren't feeling well."

"You look like a real-life princess."

Ava looked down at her prom gown and chuckled. "I suppose I do. But, alas, I am not a princess."

Gremlin wriggled free of the girl's grasp and came to the edge of the bed to greet Ava, tongue hanging halfway down to her furry knees. Starla reached over slowly and grabbed a stuffed bunny with felt horns sewn onto its head.

Ava smiled. "Whoa, cool. You have a jackalope stuffy?"

"Yeah." Starla grinned. "One day, I'm gonna have a real one. I'm gonna get him a big cage and feed him carrots."

Will looked at Ava over his shoulder and rolled his eyes in a way that his daughter couldn't see. "I told her if she could find one in the wild, she could keep it."

Ava twisted her face to keep from laughing. "Oh. That's a good plan."

"I told her they're really tough to find." Will stared at Ava like, *'play along, please.'*

"I already have a name picked out for it," Starla volunteered.

"Your numbers are very low, little lady. Did you not eat dinner?"

"It was gross."

A disapproving look crawled onto Will's face. "It was fish sticks and broccoli. It's good for you."

"I *hate* fish sticks. Miss Amy doesn't make them crunchy like you do. Hers are soggy. And the way she cooks broccoli, Dad, it smelled like a fart."

Ava snickered.

Will looked at Starla, eyebrows crinkled, lips pressed into a flat line. "Star, you gotta eat." He sighed, long and deep. "Do you want a popsicle?"

"I want ice cream."

Will rubbed his eyes so hard he saw stars. "You can have a tiny bit of ice cream, but only if you promise me next time Amy is here, you will eat your dinner."

Starla just stared at him from the depths of her pillow.

"*All* of it."

Starla nodded unconvincingly.

Will shook his head, defeated. "I'll be right back." He breezed out of the room.

Starla waved Ava closer. Ava took Will's spot on the edge of the bed.

"Can I tell you a secret?" Starla's voice was small and quiet.

Ava looked around and nodded gently.

Starla cupped a hand around her mouth and whispered, "Sometimes I don't eat dinner so that I can have juice and ice cream. Don't tell Dad."

Ava shook her head. "I gotta watch out for you. Too smart for your own good."

Starla chuckled, holding her finger over her mouth. "Gum's the word."

"I think you mean *mums the word*." Ava pretended to zip her lips and throw away the key.

Will walked back into the room with a juice box and a small bowl of strawberry ice cream. Gremlin weaseled her body toward the treat, sniffing the air wildly. As Will handed it to her, Gremlin swatted Starla's arm.

"No. Gremlin. It's mine."

Gremlins stubby snout snorted with disdain.

"Eat up, Star. We can check your levels again in a bit. If they're still low, you can have a string cheese."

Starla nodded and slurped down the contents of the juice box in a few pulls.

"Can we watch a movie?"

"No, baby. Finish your ice cream and get some rest. You can watch a movie in the morning."

"But… Daddy."

Will's eyebrows rose, and he stared at his daughter.

"Can't we… watch one of your… old movies… with Miss Ava?" Starla pouted.

Will shot Ava a look, flustered by the further delay of where they left off at the prom.

Despite Ava's longing, she would never come between a father and his child. "I mean, I'm okay with it," she said.

"Yay!" Starla croaked, rising from her pathetic display like Lazarus.

***

As the credits of *Singing in the Rain* rolled across the screen, Ava and Will looked at each other from across the couch. Starla was fast asleep, stretched across both of their laps like an accidental spacer.

Will rested his face against the back of the couch and stared at Ava. She nestled into her side similarly.

Tonight's plans were ruined but also salvaged in a sweet way.

"*Sorry tonight was a bust*," Will whispered.

"*It wasn't a bust. I got to spend it with you.*" She smiled.

Will stretched a hand out toward her. She took it. He stroked the soft flesh with his thumb.

"*I should head out,*" she whispered.

Will carefully rose from his seat, careful not to wake his daughter. "*I'll walk you out.*"

At the door, Ava swaddled herself in her coat and grabbed her rhinestone clutch. *"Tonight was—"*

Before she could utter another word, his lips found hers in the darkness, and he kissed her with passion. His body pressed her slowly against the front door with a pleasurable pressure that took the air from Ava's lungs. Her body tingled, thighs aching for his touch. He slid his hand to the nape of her neck, pulling her in closer, savoring the taste of her tongue.

They wanted more.

Needed more.

She pulled him in closer, wishing they could melt into one another as one being. Every nerve in Ava's body buzzed as she felt the bulge of his cock press against her mound through the fabric of her prom dress. Tongues explored the mouth of the other with unbridled intensity. Ava felt herself grow slick with arousal, pelvis grinding against the thigh he held between her legs.

"Daddy?"

Will and Ava stopped cold, faces burning, lungs heaving with heavy pants.

Ava looked over Will's shoulder as he pulled his thigh from between her own and readjusted his marble-hard erection.

Will was grateful for the darkness. "Hey, Star, what's up?"

"Daddy, will you tuck me in like a burrito?" A sliver of moonlight kissed the side of the young girl's face.

"Yes, baby. One second. Just let me walk Miss Ava out, and I'll be right back to tuck you in. Go get in bed. I'll be there in a second."

"Okay."

Star's little legs scurried through the house.

Ava felt a manly hand slide gently up her throat, resting there, bobbing with her pulse. His lips neared hers, hovering. She felt her nipples harden, her legs trembling.

"You are like a magnet, pulling me in, Ava."

She didn't say a word. Her clit pounded, aching, longing for him to touch her.

"It is taking every… single… *ounce* of strength that I have to not to fuck you right now."

Ava's body fell slightly slack, intentionally tightening his hand against her throat. Her breath hitched. She wanted to hike up her skirt and let him fuck her right there in the darkness against the cold front door. She needed to feel him inside of her.

His face lowered to her breasts, dragging his lips across her nipples over the fabric. They were hard as pebbles, and his cock pulsed at the thought of her arousal.

"*No bra?*" he whispered into her ear, nibbling her lobe.

Ava was breathless, barely managing the words, "No panties, either."

Will lifted the long, flowing skirt of her prom dress, inch by inch. Ava trembled against his touch, legs quivering. His hand trailed up her inner thighs, and he pressed his chest tightly to hers, hungry mouth still hovering over her parted lips. His fingers found her wet flesh, slipping gently along her soaking slit.

Ava stopped breathing.

"Mmmmm," he purred in her ear. "Is that for me?"

Ava tried to breathe, tried to speak, but could only nod. He felt her swallow hard beneath his grasp.

His finger slid deeper, and Ava rose to her tip-toes, panting in the darkness, feeling the cold knob of the door ding into her lower back.

"Before you go," he slipped his middle finger deep inside of her, feeling her damp thighs part for him, easing open to accept him, "I want another kiss."

Ava leaned forward, lunging to press her mouth to his with a fevered eagerness like nothing she'd ever felt before.

"Hmmm-nnn. No." His words were quiet, stern. He tipped her chin back so that her head touched the tiny window behind her. "Not there."

His hand released, and his body lowered. Ava's face was on fire, body trembling. She heard the rustle of fabric as he lowered to his knees and pulled her skirt over his head.

"Oh fuck…" Ava's eyes fluttered as she felt the warm, wet caress of his tongue as it slid into her pussy. He sucked gently on her clit, diving in again, pressing his lips into her flesh, lapping her up like a man parched.

She covered her mouth to keep from moaning out loud and bucked slowly against his face.

A moment later, the fabric rustled again, and he rose. She could barely make out the smile on his face as he wiped the corners of his lips. His body pressed to hers, and she juddered with deep breaths. He nudged her ear with the tip of his nose and whispered, *"Goodnight, Ava. Get home safe."*

24

Ava pulled up to the front of Will's house, equipped with her lowest-cut V-neck shirt and a bottle of wine, hoping to spend some time gazing into those blue eyes of his. After a sleepless night and a long day of unsuccessful job interviews, she needed comfort. Needed stolen kisses in the hallway. Needed the eye contact that made her want to tremble.

So when Will invited her over for dinner, she jumped at the opportunity, no longer caring if her lack of hesitancy seemed a little desperate or eager. After what he'd done to her after the charity prom, she needed more.

She loved the rush she got from knowing he wanted *her*, too. It was all-consuming, addictive, and incredibly sexy.

The street was quiet. Most had settled into their warm homes away from the blistering winds. The night sky was wide open, allowing an unimpeded view of the millions of brilliant stars that sat like a dusting of glitter on a blanket of black.

She grabbed the unopened bottle of pinot noir from the passenger seat and stepped out. She looked up at the house and froze. On the stoop stood a woman, one a similar age as Ava. The woman was talking to Will, hands stuffed into the pockets of her tattered jeans.

Will stared at Ava, still talking to the woman, face creased with annoyance and frustration. Ava got out but stayed by her Denali.

"Everything… okay here?"

"Yes," Will said curtly, leading the woman off the porch with a gentle hand. "She was just *leaving*."

A wash of jealousy and anger bubbled to the surface, displaying on Ava's face like a movie on a theater screen. "Who is she?"

Before Will could answer, the woman pivoted quickly, spinning out of his grasp and bolting back into the house.

Will scrambled to grab her. "Goddammit!"

But the wily woman was through the door already, shouting, "Star?"

Will chased the woman inside.

"What the hell…?" Ava followed with caution. Once inside, she watched Will disappear down a hallway and gritted her teeth. She was a *fool* to think someone like Will would want to be monogamous. They hadn't technically said they were exclusive, but part of her still felt betrayed.

She assumed they had something uniquely intimate, but suddenly, she wondered if she was just one of many.

In a haze of anger, Ava rounded the corner.

Will stood, gripping the shoulders of the woman, just outside of Starla's bedroom. Ava watched the flurry of waving hands and arms and heard the stream of whispered yells.

"And who the fuck is *she,* Will?" The woman growled, face contorting to a look of disgust.

"She's none of your business! Nothing in this house is your business," Will whispered.

Will grabbed her by the arm and tugged her down the hall and into the kitchen. Beneath the warm pendant lights, Ava finally saw the woman clearly. Her face hosted gaunt features, sunken cheeks, and black rings around her eyes. Her skin was pockmarked with scabs, divots, and scars. Her rumpled T-shirt hung loose on the emaciated form beneath. In the light, irritated track marks painted a clearer picture of the woman's life.

"What's going on? Who is she?" Ava asked. Her burning stare bore into Will, demanding an answer.

Eyes pinched closed, he clenched his jaw. "This is… *Sarah.*"

"I'm Starla's mother! Who the fuck are *you,* bitch?" The woman looked like she was ready to attack, the look on her face fierce and wild.

Ava took a step back into the living room, anger slowly dissipating.

"I want to see my fucking daughter!" the woman howled.

"I won't let her see you like this, Sarah." Will pointed to the red markings in the crook of her arm.

"Pfft. Those are fucking old." She waved her hand, "I've been clean for months."

"Bullshit, those are fresh, Sarah! You don't even have *a coat,* for God's sake. It's freezing out there!"

"I'm immune to the cold. It's *invigorating.*" She lunged at him with a smile. Her teeth were chipped, each stained the color of mustard.

"Jesus, Sarah, you're a *mess.* I don't want her to remember you like this. *You* shouldn't *either.* Get clean, and then we can talk."

"I'm her *mother.* A girl needs a mother."

"You signed over your rights! You have no right to be here!"

Ava couldn't help but stare, standing at the entrance to the kitchen with a bottle of wine, at a loss for what to say.

Will looked at Ava. "I'm sorry you had to see this." He turned back to Sarah. "Get sober.

Go to meetings, Sarah. When you get that six-month chip, we'll talk about visitation, okay? But right now, she's doing her language homework with her headphones on, and I won't have her knowing you showed up like this. I need you to *leave*."

"I want to see my daughter!"

"Do you really want her to see you like this? Pupils the size of dimes? Lookin' like you haven't showered in weeks? Is *this* how you want your daughter to know you?"

Sarah's eyes filled with tears. "She's *all* I fucking *have*, William!"

"So *quit*," he growled.

Sarah pressed her tongue against her cheek and shook her head at the ceiling. "You're a real piece'a work, you know that?"

Sarah started to storm out and stopped when she was level with Ava. "And I don't want *this* cunt pretending to be her *mom*." She looked back at Will. "Starla has one mother. And that's *me*."

"D-daddy, who's that?"

All six adult eyes whipped to the source of the noise in the hallway.

Ava looked at Will. "I got it. You take care of this." She pointed to Sarah and then hurried down the hall to Will's daughter.

"Baby!" Sarah said, stepping toward the girl.

"Absolutely not." Will darted in front of her.

Ava whisked Starla into her room and shut the door.

"Miss Ava? Who is that?" Starla asked.

Ava kneeled down in front of the girl. "Hey, sweetie. She's just a friend of your Dad's."

"She looked… scary."

"No, she wasn't scary." Ava thought fast. "You know what's really scary?"

Starla shook her head.

"Vampires!" Ava curled her index fingers by her face like giant vampire fangs.

Starla tried to fight the smile. "I don't like vampires."

"Oh." Ava heard the front door slam aggressively.

"I like *werewolves*!"

"Werewolves?!"

Sarah's frantic screams bellowed outside, growing quieter with every step. Starla looked out her window toward the source of the noise and then back at Ava.

"Yeah, like the *Wolfman* movie I saw." Starla howled. "Awwoooooooo!"

In tandem, they howled together like wolves.

Will opened the door and leaned against the frame, managing a smile. "What the world is going on in here?"

"I'm the *Wolfman*! *Awwooooo!*" Starla shouted.

"Yeah, we are werewolves, can't you tell?" Ava winked back at him.

"I see." His expression softened.

"Is that lady sick?" Starla inquired.

Will sighed and looked at the plush carpet. "Sort of."

"I hope she gets better."

"I do, too," Will mumbled. "C'mon. Dinner should be ready in a minute. Come get washed up, kiddo."

"Okay!" Starla scurried off.

Ava rose and looked at Will. "Are you okay?"

He stared at the ground, shrugging gently. His eyes seemed so pained.

Ava's heart ached at the sight of it. She caressed his cheek with her hand, and his eyes finally lifted to hers.

"I'm sorry you had to see that."

She smiled and shrugged. "Life is messy."

"Yes, it is." Will snickered and pressed a gentle kiss to her forehead.

He pulled back and held out a hand. She took it.

"Come on. Let's eat," he said. "I don't know about you, but I need a glass of that wine."

25

"Do you still have feelings for her?"

Will shook his head. "No. Not even a little."

"My Dad," Ava's eyes turned cold, having become a movie screen, with childhood pain as its feature attraction, "was addicted to opiates. After he had back surgery when I was a kid, he started taking them one at a time, as prescribed, *at first*. Then, he started taking two at a time, chasin' 'em down with a beer... or *three*. He started asking my family for *theirs* if they had procedures. Once that fizzled out, he straight-up found a dealer. He made his choices, too, just like Sarah. Even when we called him out about it, he never changed. We tried to get him help. He wanted none of it. The last time I saw him alive, he was passed out in his car at my wedding reception, a bottle of pills in his lap."

Will's eyes trained on her face.

Her expression was placid. "He died of an overdose a few years later."

Will didn't blink. "Ava, I'm sorry."

"Addiction is a hell of a thing. Makes you turn into someone nobody recognizes. It's too late for him, but at least your ex still has a chance. I think you did the right thing, turning her away like that. Star doesn't need to see her like that. If she can pull herself out of it, then she'll be one of the lucky ones."

"Yeah, well, I fully expected skid marks and taillights from you after that little display. You'd be right to leave and wipe your hands of the drama."

"No skid marks. No tail lights. I'm right here."

He grinned and shifted closer to her. "You are as brave as you are beautiful." He set his wine glass down, neared her face, and stared down at her lips with desire.

The feel of his body so close to hers made Ava feel like all blood had drained from her head and converged between her thighs.

Spellbound, he ran his fingers along her chin, pressing his thumb to her lower lip.

Wrapping both of her hands around it, she gently guided his thumb between her lips, whirling her tongue around the callous flesh, guiding it into the hot depths of her mouth.

Will's breath went ragged, and the suction sent a whirlwind of need straight down to his cock, now on the rise, pressing against the fabric of his tight blue jeans, aching to be unleashed.

He replaced his thumb with his tongue, driving it deep into the wet furnace that was her mouth. He kissed her with fervor, with passion, pulling her body closer to his with greedy hands.

Ava unbuttoned his pants, struggled with the zipper, and drove her hand beneath the restrictive fabric to grip his hardened cock. She smiled against his lips, intoxicated by his arousal.

Will groaned into her mouth. Desire mounted, and he pulled Ava until she was straddling him on the couch, grinding against his erection. Ava slithered from his lap to the floor, squirming between his legs, hands tugging at his pants. Will lifted his hips and hooked both thumbs beneath his underwear.

Suddenly, the *squeak* of a door hinge was followed by the patter of small feet with clicking claws.

Will's eyes widened. They froze. The creak of the door could only mean one thing:

Starla was up.

Ava jumped to her feet. Will tugged his pants back up and buttoned them quickly. They darted to different sides of the couch as Starla shuffled into the living room, rubbing sleep out of her eyes.

Will quickly pulled a throw pillow onto his lap.

"Daddy? I can't sleep." Starla pouted. "What if that weird lady comes back?"

Ava wiped a lock of sweaty red-brown hair from her face, trying her best not to look disheveled.

Will and Ava gave a look to one another, one of painful exasperation, and Ava patted the couch cushion between them. "Come, let's watch a movie."

Starla smiled gleefully and plopped onto the seat between them. Gremlin hopped up and lazily sprawled across her lap.

26

"Holy shit, I'd have mounted him right there." Madison's voice snickered through the phone.

Ava stopped brushing her teeth long enough to shout into the speakerphone, mouth full of white foam. "What was I supposed to do? His daughter came out just when things were getting heated up. I'm not gonna just jump the guy right there in the living room the second his daughter passes out again."

"Why not? I woulda!" Madison chuckled. "Man, girl, you gotta nut up or shut up. You think you can just whine to me and not do something to change it, then you've come to the *wrong* friend."

Ava spit into the basin. "I'm not *whining*."

Madison remained silent on the other side of the phone.

"Shit. Okay, fine. Maybe I'm whining a *little*."

"You should go see him today. Like during the day, when his kid's at school, so she can't cock-block y'all. If you can't get time alone with him at his house, tackle him in that truck! I'm sure the seats go back."

"Madison, I am an *adult*. I don't fuck in vehicles anymore. I'm a grown-ass woman."

"Dude, banging in a truck is hot! Especially when it's all snowy outside. Fog up the windows… it's like passionate."

"It's cramped, is what it is."

"Do you wanna ride the bologna pony or what? I'm offering you solutions to your problems. Putnam said he's cleaning her house today. Heard her bragging about it last week at the bar when she was downing her stupid gin and tonics."

"I'm pretty sure he's at Putnam's house today. She was bragging to me about it last week. That woman is who I hope to be when I'm grown up. You should go over there. Wear a dress. No underwear -- for easy access -- and ambush him in his truck after. Test the shocks on that bitch."

"Putnam? As in Lena Putnam? The chick over by the mountain whose husband owns that modular closet company?"

"Yeah. I *idolize* that bitch."

"Why?" Ava started applying makeup in the mirror.

"Because even at 56, that woman gets more dick than a urinal. I've got *rookie* numbers compared to her."

"Set your goals higher, Madison," Ava teased.

"You might be happy being tethered to one cock for the rest of your life. For me, variety is the spice of life."

"*Fine*," Ava relented. "I'll go see him today."

"Yesss! Atta girl!" Madison dropped her phone and picked it up again. "Whoops!"

"You alright over there?"

"Yeah, I'm always dropping this fucking thing like a bar 'a soap in a prison shower."

Ava shook her head, plucking the mascara out of a cubby on her counter.

"Have you told him about what you're doing for him?"

"No, and don't you blab. It's still in the works."

"It's not too late to abort that plan, Harla. I still think it's too much."

"Well, I think he's going to like it."

Madison sighed. "Ooooo-kayyyyy."

27

The memories of last night simmered on the back burner of his mind, threatening to boil over. Even after a full night of sleep and a cold shower, the thoughts of Ava grinding on his lap, hands buried beneath his jeans, massaging his cock, blazed a trail through his brain.

The pain of the too-tight suspenders digging into his shoulders anchored him back to reality. He was cleaning the stove housed in Lena Putnam's farmhouse-style kitchen in little more than soaked fireman's pants and hat. Sweat glistened off his bare shoulders and abs as he used elbow grease to remove charred bits of food from one of the burners.

"Francesca makes such a mess, doesn't she?" Lena asked from her perch on the counter. Her leathery cleavage and overdone face full of makeup seemed off-putting beneath her recessed lights.

Will continued to scrub away, faking a smile to his most loyal customer. "She can be as messy as she wants. That's what I'm here for. "

"You're here for more than just toiling away with a scouring pad, and you know it. *Any* dipshit can scrub my burners, William. I'm paying to watch that sculpted body." She groaned like she was eating something delicious.

"Oh, please. You haven't been down on your hands and knees in, what, a decade or so?" he teased.

"On the *contrary,* my love. It's one of my favorite positions to *be* in." She winked.

He shook his head. "You're such a flirt." He rinsed the scouring pad in the sink. "When is Mr. Putnam coming back from his trip to Japan? I thought he was due home yesterday."

"He was, but they had to iron out some of the fine print. Something about adverse side effects, I honestly stopped listening." Mrs. Putnam hopped down from the counter and leaned against the cabinet beside the stove, crossing her arms in a not-so-subtle attempt to hoist her cleavage.

"When are we gonna stop playing games and get down to it? I know this is allegedly a look-but-don't-touch service, but everyone's got a price, William. What's yours?" She gently pinched his ass.

Will jumped, smile fading in an instant. "The rules haven't *changed,* Lena." He pointed a sponge at her, speaking tersely, "You *know* better."

"Why can't we have a little fun?" She pouted dramatically, reminding him of a character from *Gone with the Wind.*

"Do you know what they call paying for sex while I'm on the clock?"

"'*Worth it?*'" she joked.

He was less-than-amused. "*Prostitution.*"

Lena looked dejected, leaning her slight frame against the pristine cabinets. "Oh, come on, Willy." She pouted again. "I won't tell anyone. It can be our little secret."

"*I* would know, Mrs. Putnam. That's not what I am here for. So, you can either enjoy the show and how clean your home is after, or I can leave. Your choice."

"So *stern.*" Lena teased, "I like it when a man bosses me around like that."

Will's eyes dropped to the stove, and he fought the urge to walk out.

"How much for just a little bare-assed spanking?" Lena shrugged. "It can be you *or* me. I'll take what I can get."

Will fought to keep a pleasant smile on his face.

Lena huffed. "Who is she?"

"Who?"

"Oh, come on, Willy. I'm sure there's *someone* if you have the balls to turn down money being in *this* line of work. Is it Marsha? She's always been one for whoring around."

"There is someone. Nobody you know. She doesn't run in your circles."

Mrs. Putnam crossed her arms. "Does she know what you *do* for a living?"

"Of course." He started scrubbing again.

"And she's… just… what… *fine* with it?"

"Yep." Will took a wet rag from the counter and wiped down the area around the cook-top.

"Does your boss have any fresh meat he could send me? Maybe someone a little more eager to play ball? I'm getting rather bored of this game."

"I *am* the boss, Mrs. Putnam. It's a one-man operation."

Lena leaned in toward Will and grabbed the crotch of his fireman's pants.

Will jumped back. "Lena!"

She laughed. "Oh, come on. I was only playing around."

Will snatched up the cleaning supplies and dumped them in the sink with a clatter. "Mrs. Putnam, I warned you not to cross the line."

He waltzed toward the front door, plucked his coat off the rack, and grabbed the knob. Lena grabbed his shoulder.

"Wait, where are you going? I paid you for three hours. You can't just leave. Willy, I'm sorry. I took it too far! Charles hasn't touched me in months. I got carried away."

"Mrs. Putnam, you *know* the rules, and yet, you *continue* to break them. Find another cleaning service."

"Oh, come on. You're not walking out in the middle of a job, are you?"

"Mrs. Putnam, I'm firing you as a client," Will growled before opening the door and making his way out to the stoop.

"Fine. It isn't prostitution if I don't *pay* you for it. And since I'm no longer your client..." Lena grabbed his jaw and whipped his face toward her, planting her lips on his.

Will jerked away, appalled. "What the *hell* has gotten into you, Lena?!"

Out of the corner of his eye, he saw a black Denali — *Ava's black Denali* —idling in front of the house he was fleeing. His stomach flipped as he saw the look of horror on Ava's face through the window. Her eyes were wide, jaw ajar, with an expression of utter shock.

As she registered the scene, her expression warped to fury.

Dammit! What the fuck was Ava doing here?

How did she know where I was?

How much of that did she see?!

Will bolted toward the street. "Ava! That was not—"

The tires squelched in the snow, spinning and struggling to gain traction. Ava was distraught, body rocking as she jammed the accelerator repeatedly, only to feel it lose traction again.

Will ran to her window and rapped his fist frantically on the glass. "Ava, please, just listen," Will yelled.

Ava's eyes flashed fire as she let off of the foot pedal before punching the accelerator once again. This time, the tires caught, finally gaining traction. The Denali roared away, flinging snow at Will's calves.

With tears welling in her eyes, Ava sped down the snowy block and out of sight.

Will looked up at Lena Putnam and then back in the direction Ava had sped off. "*Fuck!*"

28

Ava's phone rang yet again, and she sent the call to voicemail.

The screen lit up with a notification: *11 missed calls.* Will was persistent; she would give him that.

She knew what he did for a living, but as he stood in that doorway, bare-chested, kissing a woman he allegedly worked for, it broke Ava. She felt foolish for believing he offered a purely legitimate service. It all made sense now why Will was able to keep his hands to himself for so long…

Ava wasn't the only woman in his life.

Watching him kiss Lena Putnam was the final straw. One cheater had already insidiously snuck his way into her life. She learned that lesson in the hardest way imaginable. She wasn't about to get entangled with a man she'd have to worry about like that.

Mrs. Putnam had fake breasts and an even faker personality.

If that's the kind of woman Will wanted, so be it.

Ava was all natural.

A natural disaster… but natural nonetheless.

A fist rapped at the door. Ava reluctantly pulled up the camera feed on her phone.

It was Will, fully dressed in a button-down shirt and khakis.

Ava pushed the microphone button. "Go away, Will."

"You're not answering my calls. Ava, please let me explain what you saw. If you hear me out and still don't want to talk to me, I'll leave you alone, I promise."

Ava growled, "If it'll get you to stop blowing up my damned *phone*, then fine." She stormed to the front door and swung it open, gesturing halfheartedly for him to enter.

Will walked inside and moved a pile of unfolded clothes from the couch to clear a place to sit. Ava stood.

Will looked around. "I still *really* need to finish cleaning your house."

"Don't worry about *my house*. Speak! Make it fast."

Will swallowed hard. "I'm sorry you saw that today. I promise you that is not how my customers act."

"Clearly, that's how at least *one* acts," Ava snarled. "God knows how many others."

"I fired her, Ava. Right before she wrenched my face like that and laid one on me. She propositioned me, and I fired her. I was leaving two hours early when you saw me."

Ava crossed her arms and grimaced.

"Mrs. Putnam kissed me. I didn't kiss her *back*. She's a lonely housewife whose husband's constantly away on business. She shouldn't have done that. That's not part of what I offer, I swear. I don't *sleep* with any of my clients. I don't *kiss* my clients—"

"You kissed *me*."

"You weren't a *client*."

Ava threw her hands up in the air. "Do you hear yourself?"

"Sometimes, yes, clients try to get a little handsy. But, I swear, I always shut it down, Ava!"

"And I'm just supposed to believe that you don't fuck *any* of them?"

"*Yes*!"

"Why?"

"Because that's fucking *prostitution*. I would *never* want to do that! And even if I *did*, I would never risk that with Starla! Where would she *go* if I got locked up for banging some married broad for money, Ava? Her mom already *abandoned* her. She's brought *enough* shame into the equation. I'm not gonna add *to it*!"

"I don't believe you."

"Ava, I need you to trust me right now."

"Why? Why should I trust you?"

"Because when you love someone, you have to be able to trust them!"

The words hung heavy in the silence between them.

"Ava, I care about you. So much. I can see myself falling for you."

Ava felt her rage fading but clung steadfastly to it. Rage kept her safe, kept her protected.

I won't fall for another cheater. Not again.

Fool me once; shame on you. Fool me twice…

"I'm not sure I believe you," she said weakly.

"Tell me how I can prove it to you. I can't prove something I haven't done. So, just tell me what I have to do."

Ava could hear his voice cracking with emotion and sincerity. She could feel her defenses crumbling. "I need some time to think."

"I'm not your ex-husband, Ava. Please, don't make me pay for his mistakes."

His words gutted her.

"I walked into your house and saw him kissing *you* and I trusted *your* explanation."

"I just need time, Will."

"Fine." He hung his head and sighed. "I understand." Will stood and turned toward the door, stopping before he reached it. "Why were you *there*, anyway? How did you know where I was?"

"It doesn't matter now."

"It matters to me."

"Madison told me you'd probably be there. I was trying to meet up with you for something."

"For *something*?"

"...To finish what we started last night."

Her eyes portrayed a deep hurt. Will's shoulders sank.

Her voice cracked. "I think you should go now, Will."

Will nodded and let himself out without another word.

Ava felt tears prick the backs of her eyes. She put her head in her palms and sobbed.

29

No missed calls. No missed texts. Nothing.

It had been five days since he'd last spoken to Ava, each feeling like a year in limbo. Will flopped his cell phone back onto the nightstand and rubbed his face in the dark, replaying the argument in his head.

He'd never seen Ava mad before. She was stubborn, unwilling to listen, and jealous. And, still, he missed her.

Fiercely.

He rolled onto his side, and a moment later, the tiny screen illuminated the room. He snatched his phone, heart racing.

One new text message. He tapped the notification, and it took him to his and Ava's text log. A new text showed at the bottom:

AVA: You up?

WILL: Yes.

AVA: Can I call you?

WILL: Absofuckinglutely.

Suddenly, his phone chimed. He swallowed hard and answered.

Silence.

"Ava?" He cleared his throat.

"Hey."

Will's heart skipped a beat at her voice. It had only been a short time, but her voice made his stomach flip with excitement.

"I want to trust you." She paused. "I just need to know I'm not being played again. I can't take another cheater, Will. I can't do it. Last time, it broke my fucking heart into a million pieces."

"I would never do that to you, Ava. I care about you. I want to be with you. But that means you need to be able to trust me. Otherwise, this will never work."

"I believe you." Ava's voice seemed quiet and uneasy.

"If you just give me the chance, I will prove it to you. With my *actions*, Ava."

Silence.

"I was wondering if we could go away together for the weekend."

He felt as if all of the air had been sucked from the room. "You know I can't do that, Ava. I have a child."

The line went silent for a moment.

"I'm sorry. It was stupid of me to even ask."

Will wanted so badly to say yes. The words bit at his tongue, begging him to release them, but he held them at bay. "I have no one who can watch her overnight. I barely trust the babysitter for a few hours. She's just a kid *herself*, pretty much."

"I know."

"I'm sort of on my own here."

"Right. I'm sorry," Ava croaked, regretting the question.

"Where were you wanting to go?"

"I was going to take you to Salem." She quickly corrected herself, "Oregon, not Massachusetts. That would be crazy."

"Yeah," he chuckled.

"The cherry trees start blossoming soon. They do a whole festival for it. I've always wanted to go. More than anything, it was just an excuse to be alone with you."

"Well, I know it's not much, but my babysitter is free on Saturday."

"Fantastic. How about we have dinner at my place? Around seven? I'll cook you something in my now-clean kitchen." She chuckled softly.

"What a treat. I'd love that."

"It's a date."

Will swore he could hear her smile through the phone.

30

Will rang the doorbell, and Ava answered it, swinging open the door to reveal herself. His heart nearly stopped.

Ava wore a slinky dress. The red fabric hugged her curves. A low, plunging neckline showcased her cleavage. The slit up the side put her smooth, moisturized legs on display.

"Wow." It was all Will could think of to say. Beneath his jacket, he wore a deep blue button-down and pressed slacks.

She beckoned playfully with a finger, and he followed her inside. He looked around, hanging his coat on the hook by the door.

The house had been cleaned. No clothing on the furniture, floors swept, surfaces dusted. It looked like a different home.

"Wow, again." Will looked at the spot on the wall where her torn wedding photo used to hang, now replaced by a tasteful paint-by-number of a blossoming, pink Kwanzan cherry tree in a frame.

"Did you paint this?" He pointed to it.

"Sure did. I'm a regular Picasso."

"Is it new?"

"It is. I don't know if you know this, but I recently lost my job and have a lot of free time on my hands as of late."

He laughed and bobbed his head, looking around. "Something smells amazing."

"I'm making ziti. Family's recipe."

Will took a sniff of the air and turned to Ava. "No. That's not it."

"No?" Ava asked.

Will walked closer, wrapping his arms around her lower back and tugging her to him. "No, it's…" He nuzzled her neck and groaned in her ear. "It's definitely *you*."

Ava felt petals of warmth unfurl in her belly as he pulled the red strap down the arch of her shoulder, following it with his lips. Ava let out an involuntary gasp.

Will scooped a hand below her ear and pulled her lips to his, kissing her with sensual abandon as the intoxicating smells of food filled the air.

Will led Ava backward onto the couch and laid her down, never taking his mouth from hers. He carefully laid her head on the plush leather and laid her back with a moan. He nestled a leg between her thighs and kneeled, pressing his body down over hers. Her face grew red, and his hand found its way back to her jaw, tilting her head back as his lips moved down to her breasts.

She gasped for air like a drowning woman as he tugged the fabric down and took her nipple softly into his eager mouth, sucking and swirling the sensitive flesh, teasing her as she gasped louder. Her body bucked up, and he nibbled and sucked, engulfing her perfect pink buds with his hot tongue.

His erection raged, fierce and angry like a lion attacking its cage, seeking freedom beyond the bars.

With his free hand, he hiked her skirt up as her back arched beneath him, responding to his every touch.

"*Please*," she begged, breathy, almost without making a sound. "*Please…*"

He felt her leg slide over the back of his, pulling him close, tightening like a boa constrictor. Her hands slid through his hair, mussing and tugging, pulling his face back to her breast for more.

"Please *what*?" he asked between languid, teasing licks of her stiffened areolas.

He pushed her further into the arm of the couch, placing his other knee between her bunched skirt, spreading her wide, pressing the lump of his covered cock against her skimpy panties, feeling the heat there.

"Please, *what*?" he repeated. "*I want to hear you say it.*"

"Please fuck me," she breathed into the ether. She needed him in the worst way, or rather, *the best way.*

Hisssssss.

The sound came from the kitchen like a steam valve opening.

"Shit," Ava panted, lurching bolt-upright on the leather. "The pasta's boiling over!" Flustered, Ava crawled out from under him and disappeared into the kitchen.

Moments later, she popped her head out, cheeks red, hair tangled. A smile spread across her face. "How about we take a time out."

Will nodded, praying the blood would rush back to his head soon.

"Ziti for dinner," she winked, "and you for dessert."

"I can get behind that."

***

As dinner wound down and red wine relaxed her, Ava pushed her bowl aside and smiled. "I have something for you."

"Is it lacy or see-through?" Will's eyes locked on hers like a predator, ready to pounce.

"No." She laughed. She rose from her seat and retrieved a thick orange packet from the hutch behind him. She placed it near the decanter and sat back down across from him. "It's a present. I hope you like it. I worked really hard on this for you."

He lifted it up and smiled. "Is it a paint-by-number?"

"No, it's way cooler than that."

Will tugged out a bound packet of paper and read the cover:

The Man Maid Business Plan.

He laughed, flipping through the fat stack of typed pages. "What… is this?"

"It's a business proposal. I've been working on it for a while now."

Will flipped to another page and nodded, not nearly as excited as she was. "Uh… huh."

Ava leaned across the table and turned some pages to the projections section, which was full of colorful charts and graphs. "So look, this is a fully fleshed-out business plan that will appeal to clients who have lots of disposable income in the Jackson Hole area and even potential investors, but best of all, if you turn to the back, you can see how easy it would be for us to eventually branch out and make it a national or worldwide chain, sort of like *Chippendales*. Actually, I modeled some of it after them."

"Us?" Will repeated, his face suddenly pale.

"Us. You." She frowned, upset that he wasn't getting excited over what she'd just given him. "Look. I'm a finance gal. Business-minded.

You need someone to keep your tax documents in order and keep an eye on expenditures and profits. That's where I come in. That way, you can focus on the actual cleaning and getting together a potential *fleet*. Then you can manage cleaners to make your money instead of doing the actual cleaning."

Silence.

She continued, trying to sell him on the idea. "According to research for similar businesses in like income areas, your profitability, not just for *gross* profit, but *net* profit is very high. With no overhead, this could eventually be a cash cow, Will. You could be making so much more. We could hire new talent to give clients some variety and not run you ragged."

"Is this about Lena Putnam?"

"What?" She was appalled at the accusation.

"Is this because you don't want me anywhere near clients because you don't trust me?"

"What? No! This is about realizing the full potential of your business." She pressed her hands into the table and tried to smile to de-escalate the situation. "I've already taken the liberty to set you up a website, got you a domain, optimized your SEO, and started your presence on the web." She smiled with desperation. "I've done some of the heavy lifting for this. This is my gift to you."

"But I didn't ask for this gift. I didn't want this gift. Ava, this is... this is a bit of an overstep."

"An overstep?" Her feelings were genuinely hurt. "Will, all you have to do is sign and file the incorporation paperwork, and you are literally in business. Officially. Legally. With the ability to expand. You can start bringing on more cleaning staff, more costumes, and providing your own cleaning solvents. I can schedule clients for you. Eventually, we could expand to other wealthy areas and major cities. The sky is seriously the limit with this, Will."

"This... this is too much." Will leaned back in his chair and pushed the packet toward her like his body was rejecting it.

Ava's heart sank. All the work and time she'd put into it...

She thought he would be *thrilled.*

Instead, he seemed genuinely pissed off.

"What about it is too much?"

"*All of it,*" Will muttered.

"I worked really hard on this."

"I'm sorry, Ava. But nobody asked you to do this. We just started dating. We haven't even slept together. Now you want to manage my business? This is my livelihood."

Ava furrowed her brows. "Yes! That's my point exactly. It's your livelihood. This time next year, you could be making ten times as much."

"Life's not all about money."

Ava reeled back, recoiling like a snake ready to strike. "I *know* that."

"I appreciate this. But… I wasn't prepared for this. I thought tonight would go differently."

"This is who I am, Will. I'm *driven*. I'm a *go-getter*. I don't just sit around and let opportunities pass by. If I see a solid investment, I'm going to do everything I can to make it thrive."

"I *see* that."

Ava felt defeated.

All that time. All the research. All of the effort.

Wasted.

After sitting together in silence for a long moment, Ava finally found enough voice to speak. "I think it's probably time for you to go."

"Okay." Will rose slowly, grabbed the packet, and headed for his coat. As he put it on, he spoke again, not making eye contact with her. "Thank you for dinner. It was delicious."

Ava didn't say a word. She sat at the table, stunned, as the door opened and closed quietly.

31

Will flipped through the packet in bed, skimming the financial projections and the suggested goalposts. The gift, though overbearing, was a truly thoughtful effort. It was clear by the care poured into every page that Ava believed in him and wanted him to succeed. There was passion there, faith in him, faith in what he was doing with his life.

But was it really what he wanted: decades of cleaning in policeman uniforms like a stripper with a sponge?

The stack of paper forced him to think about the questions he'd been carefully avoiding.

True, it was no small feat to have paid his home off and steadily be working toward his daughter's college fund.

But was this what he wanted to be?

Would it eventually embarrass Starla?

His looks would eventually fade -- *though many women did seem to appreciate a silver fox these days*. He was well aware of the ticking clock limiting his future in nearly-naked cleaning.

Ava was right.

It was a profitable idea to expand to a fleet.

Another thing weighing on his mind was that he wasn't sure Ava entirely trusted him. The way she spoke about organizing his life, essentially running it *for* him, made him feel like a child again with a dominant, bossy parental figure.

Still… thinking back to the hurt on her face, he couldn't shake the feeling that he might be wrong and that maybe it was simply a genuine, good-hearted gesture meant to bolster his career.

He *thunked* his head against the headboard.

You pushed away a woman you care about for what? Pride? Ego?

Fear?

The last thought stuck to his brain like an indelible stain.

He glanced at his phone. His heart leaped when a text notification showed up on his home screen.

And it stopped when he realized it was from his best friend, Barrett.

BARRETT: How's it going? Have you given your girl the old hot beef injection yet?

Will slumped down in his bed and pulled the covers over his head, fighting the urge to groan.

32

"Spill it. I want all the details. But you gotta hurry, my break is only fifteen minutes. Some of us work, you know," Madison teased and then yelled at someone on the other end of the phone.

"Thanks for that," Ava spat sarcastically, shaking her head at no one as she lay draped across her couch. Her cell was on the arm of the couch, and as Ava looked at it, she transported back to Will's hand pinning her there, cock grinding between her thighs, tightened breast in his mouth…

"How was it? Scratch that, how *big* was it?"

Ava balled a fist and smacked it to her forehead, wincing. "We never got that far."

"What?! I thought you got a bikini wax and everything yesterday? You were *ready*! What happened?"

"I messed things up."

Madison was silent for a few beats. "Oh God. You didn't."

"I did, Madison."

"Girl, tell me you didn't give him that business plan."

Silence.

"Ava!" Madison growled. "No! Whyyyyyyy? I told you that was a dumb idea."

"Yeah, well…" Ava wanted to say that Madison's intuition couldn't be trusted, that she was a fool. But that would be the pot calling the kettle black.

"Please tell me you didn't do the whole binder thing with the timelines and a fucking *projector*."

"No." Ava said sternly, "No binder. No projector. I knew that would be too much."

"Harla, listen to me, hun. I mean this in the nicest possible way, but you fucked up. You planned this guy's life out for him before he even fucked you silly. That's cat-five-clinger stuff, babe. I know you're rusty at the whole dating thing, but people don't even call each other boyfriend girlfriend anymore til they've dated for months, much less plot out their entire *future* with graphs."

"You're right."

"You had one task last night, and that was to get your clam rammed."

"Oh, for the love of God…"

"Now, what *exactly* did he say?"

"He said I was trying to control him, that I didn't trust him, and that I overstepped."

"Check, check, and check, baby girl."

It felt like a punch to the gut. "I'm *not* controlling!"

"Oh, *please.*"

"If he'd have asked you to do this or even *hinted* at it, I'd say he's in the wrong. But you can't just pitch a guy the rest of his life and a plan for all of his finances without scaring the living shit out of him."

Ava groaned, pinching the bridge of her nose to keep the tears at bay. "How do I fix it, Maddy? Is it fixable?"

Madison clicked her tongue against the roof of her mouth. "Harla, you can always try. There is no harm in going back to him and saying, 'Look, I messed up. I overstepped with my big feet, and I'm sorry.' But it's important to remember that there are plenty of other cocks in the sea, Okay?"

"Why'd you have to add the big feet thing in there? That's just unnecessarily *hurtful.*"

"Toughen up, buttercup. You and those big ass feet gotta get steppin'. Go reach out. Text him. Call him. Just… don't just be a creep and show up at his house. Next time you see him, wear a push-up bra. Since you lost the postdivorce weight, your boobs look sad in them granny-bras you wear."

"Wow. That's Madison."

"Remember… underwire and padding. Gotta go, bitch. I love you."

"I love you, too." Ava clicked the end call button and stared at the cherry blossom background on her phone for a moment, picturing herself far away, in a place without business proposals or padded bras where the flowers rained down over her in a slow shower of soft pink petals.

33

"What do you think?" Will sat at the counter in his kitchen. The rigid wooden stool dug into his hips as he finished the last of his cappuccino.

"I think…" Barrett scratched his head of thick black hair and made a face, "I think this actually looks fucking *legit*." He adjusted on his stool and slapped the packet of papers onto the granite. "The girl knows her shit."

"Fuck." Will shook his head in frustration.

"She just… *did* this for you? You didn't, like, ask her or anything?"

Will shook his head.

Barrett tugged at his tight T-shirt and crossed his tanned, bulging arms, toned from practically *living* at the gym since his divorce two years prior. "Weird."

"Right?"

Barrett opened it again, flipping through line graphs and pie charts. He rubbed his chiseled jaw. "You could take this to a bank and get a loan with this. She thought of everything, man. Down to the cost of storage for your cleaning products and Windex by the gallon. She put a lot of time into this. Most people would charge—"

"I *know*." Will softly tapped his fist on the counter. "I've read that thing like 1000 times over the last week."

Barrett itched his stubble. "You fucked up."

"What?"

"I said you fucked up. I'd love it if a chick made some fucking sense of my life. I'm like a wayward stray. I'm like one of those dogs you just see wandering around in Mexico in the streets. Shit… now that you blew it, you mind if I gave her a go?"

"Hell *yes,* I'd *mind,*" Will snarled. "What the fuck is *wrong* with you?"

Barrett giggled. "Dude, you have *feelings* for her. You'd never snap at me like that over any of the *other* girls. You're usin' this to drive a wedge because you're scared."

Will folded over in his seat and laid his forehead on the granite countertop. He moaned.

"She's not Sarah, man. She's like whatever the antithesis of Sarah is, seems like. You know, not every woman's gonna run off and leave you high and dry with a kid. This chick has invested her time and effort into you, Will. And I think *that* freaks you out."

"Well, it's too late now."

"No, it's *not*." Barrett bared his straight, white teeth in a wide smile. "You're makin' it sound worse than it is. Just *talk to her*. Tell her you're an idiot. Let her know this was a little much but that you appreciate what she was tryin' to do. You gotta stop this stupid game."

"What *game*?"

"The one where the second a girl shows a real interest in you, you find some reason to bolt."

Will rinsed his mug and set it in his dish drainer. He stayed silent, unsure how to respond. Barrett was right, but he didn't want to admit it. Barrett's swollen head barely fit through the door frame as it was.

Swigging down the rest of his coffee, Barrett smacked his lips and stood from his stool. "I gotta go, man. Got to go to work."

"What are you doing tonight? Wanna come over? Do a board game night?"

"No-can-do, *mi amigo*. Got a date with a crazy hot stewardess. At least one of us knows how to get laid these days."

"Shut up." Will laughed.

"Fuuuuuuuck, it's gonna be a good night."

Will's phone vibrated across the counter. Both men stared at it for a moment and then glanced at each other.

Barrett looked at the screen. "Who is Carla O'Neil?"

"Client." Will looked worried, eyes large. He pushed the speakerphone button. "Mrs. O'Neil?"

"Will?" She was crying hard, sobs muffled by her hands. "Things… have gotten worse. He… laid hands on my son. We are locked in a bathroom right now."

Will stared up at Barrett, jaw clenched tight.

"Remember when you said I could call you for a ride if I was ready to leave?"

"Yes."

"Well," she sobbed, "how soon can you be here?"

34

Seventeen minutes after the call, Will slammed the truck into park in front of Carla's home. Barrett followed close behind in his obsidian Jeep, crunching to a stop in a pile of snow right behind him. Both men leaped out of their vehicles, Will with a solemn face, Barrett with the crazed giddiness of a school bully about to pound a weakling.

Barrett bounced lightly on his feet, tennis shoes compacting the snow up the sidewalk as Will walked slowly, fists balled by his sides.

"No ass-kicking," Will warned. "I'm not sending Starla into the fuckin' system goin' to *jail* over this guy."

"Speak for yourself. I have no obligations. Some light bitch slapping might be in order."

"That's still assault."

"Not if I get him to hit me *first*."

"What if he has a gun?"

"This is *Wyoming*." Barrett laughed. "Of *course,* he has a gun. Probably got a bunch of 'em. That doesn't mean he's gonna *use* it. Plus, I brought my own." He grabbed both coat-covered biceps, one at a time. "And *these guns* are rated 'E for everyone.' Mr. O'Neil, meet Smith… and Wesson."

"Cooler heads prevail here." Will looked at the wooden front door with a mosaic glass window, one he'd walked through more than twenty times already. Shapes inside shifted, darting left and right.

He turned back to Barrett, "You remember how we got you into Mason's party that one time?"

A grin spread across Barrett's face. "The good old E.W.?"

Will nodded.

SMASH!

Both of their attention snapped to the door as the glass mosaic exploded outward in a spray of colored glass. An object missed their faces narrowly, hurtling out into the cold air. Will and Barrett watched the full jar of pickles explode like a green firework on the snowy walkway behind them. The men hunched down, careful to avoid any other thrown projectiles.

Barrett crouched beneath the hole in the door. "Sir? Mr. O'Neil? Someone is breaking into your car!" His powerful voice bellowed through the neighborhood.

"What?!" A man's voice shouted from inside, rising above Carla's muffled screams. "Goddammit—"

Will wrenched open the doorknob, and both men slammed their body weight against it in unison, like battering rams. The combined force knocked the abusive prick inside to the tile floor.

Will and Barrett stormed inside. Carla screamed, her children cowering behind her in fear in the hallway, busted glass laid at their feet. Carla's face was bruised and soaked with tears, lip busted. One of her eyes was already starting to swell shut, and a red handprint graced her throat. Her left arm hung at an odd angle by her side. Will had no doubt that if left alone, the man would have killed her.

Carla's cries of relief were gut-wrenching when she saw the men.

Will recognized the man's face from the pictures he'd dusted around the house. Frank O'Neil. *What a piece of shit.*

Frank groaned on the floor, trying his damnedest to stand. Will dove, grabbing Frank's legs and latching them together with his arms.

"Go upper!" Will shouted.

Barrett was all too happy to oblige, pinning Frank's arms to the floor with his knees and sinking his full weight down.

Frank screamed.

Will looked back. "Carla, you and the kids get in either of the vehicles outside. Hurry!"

"You're not fucking going *anywhere*!" Frank yowled, trying to wrestle his limbs free from the men. "Your fat ass is *worthless* without me, and you know it! You got nowhere to go! You are fucking *nothing*!"

"Shut up!" Barrett slapped the back of the man's head so hard that his face bounced off the tile.

Carla's battered face flashed red with anger. "You... will never... see us... *again,*" she growled.

Barrett turned his face up toward Carla with a sly grin, "You want a free shot? I'll hold him down for you."

She shook her head. "No." Carla spit on the back of Frank's head, and he thrashed in anger.

Carla and the kids made their way out of the shattered front door. They scuttled through the snow and piled in Will's truck.

Frank tugged his arm free and swung wild, landing a punch right across Barrett's jaw. Barrett reeled back, grimacing in pain, ears ringing.

"Barrett, are you okay?" Will asked, whipping Frank's arm back at a wrong angle until the man cried out.

"You done fucked up throwing the first punch." Barrett laughed. "Now it's my turn." He looked at Will. "Let him go. Get to the truck. Get the wife and kids out of here. I'll handle *him*."

"I'm not just going to *leave*."

Barrett laughed casually as if they weren't all in the middle of a shit-storm. "Go. I got this all day."

Will thought for a moment, debating his options, and then fled fast back to the truck. Barrett released Frank's hands, and the second the abuser got to his feet, Barrett plowed his fist into his nose with a satisfying crunch. Frank wailed through the blood, clutching his face.

"Yeah, I guess it *is* fun hitting little *bitches*, Frankie!"

Barrett raised a booted foot and kicked the living shit out of Frank. Frank tumbled back, skidding across the glass on the floor toward the kitchen.

Barrett lumbered over to Frank as the man tried to push himself up out of the blood-smeared glass. Barrett slammed a boot against his back, shoved Frank's chest to the floor, and yanked his wallet out of the man's slacks. He slapped the back of Frank's balding head with it. "*Asshole tax*."

Not wasting any time, Barrett waved, and Will stopped the truck in the middle of the street.

Barrett clomped over to it. Carla rolled down the window.

"Here. Y'all are married, right?"

Carla nodded solemnly, tears streaming.

"Good. *Community property.*" Barrett walked back toward his Jeep and waved cheerfully.

Will sped off, not stopping until Carla and the kids were somewhere safe.

35

Ava stared long and hard at the colored creme paint in its little lidded cup, the same cobalt blue of Will Jessup's eyes. She dipped her paintbrush in and swirled it, disturbing the unwelcome hold it had over her. The television quietly displayed CCTV footage of the last time a victim had been seen alive before his brutal slaying in 2006. The lead detective spoke in a recent interview, his voice grabbing her attention like a vice. He sounded just like Will. She glanced up, but the man's face was weathered and mustached. Ava's brush hesitated over the numbered shape on her piece. *How can someone be out of your life and yet still seem like they're everywhere?*

She returned her focus to the paint-by-number of a churning ocean wave and sighed loudly. Kuda perked up from his dog bed to look at her.

"I'm too distracted to paint, Kuda."

She snapped her paint cup closed to seal the air out and took the rinse mug filled with mocha-colored water to the kitchen. Kuda trotted closely behind. She put the cup in the sink and scanned the room for something worth doing.

Days had passed without a word from Will. No text. No call. No knock at the door.

Just annoying silence.

Just then, the dryer buzzed.

Thank God. Something to do.

Too stubborn to find a hamper, she carried the laundry to her bedroom in her arms, dropping stray items like breadcrumbs from the hefty heap. Kuda snatched up a red, lacy push-up bra and followed behind, ever the helper.

She plopped down the laundry on the bed she'd done a half-assed job of making. Thoughts of Will oozed from the recesses of her brain. Like a bulging dam about to burst, they trickled in, reminding her of his warm voice, the feel of his fingers slipping between her legs, those *damn* blue eyes… she couldn't get him out of her mind.

She stormed to her walk-in closet and tugged open the door, flicking on the overhead light. One by one, she snatched the hangers from the railing, trying to focus on her search instead of the barrage of thoughts. Tears pricked her eyes, and suddenly she felt furious.

Goddammit… she tried to *help*, not *control* him.

Or had she? Had some part of her wanted to line things up in a way that would offer more protection for her own heart?

Sure, she had trust issues, but how was trying to *help him* so severely misconstrued? She felt within reach of everything she ever wanted and somehow ended up… with *nothing*.

She put the last of her clothes away, tears forming behind her eyes like rain clouds. She wandered to the empty bed, remembering the night he lay beside her. She laid down, cuddling the pillow he'd used. The pillowcase had since been washed, but she could have sworn she could still faintly make out his scent.

36

Ava strolled into the three-story, weather-worn building. Today was the day that everything would turn around.

She could *feel* it.

She was going to take life by the balls and squeeze until it surrendered. Her heels echoed through the walls of the lobby. Tile swirled in a flowery pattern on the floor. The front desk was back-lit, giving the administrative assistant a glow like an angel.

Her sweet face was framed by shoulder-length blonde hair pinned back at the temples. "Can I help you?"

"Yes, I'm here for an interview with Mr. Carlin."

"Oh!" the woman bounced, typing on her keyboard stationed below the countertop. "Alright. He is aware you are here. You can have a seat over there." She gestured to an area with black chairs flanked by two leggy, potted Bird-of-Paradise plants.

Beyond the benches, in an office with clear walls, a middle-aged man sat behind a metal desk. His squared goatee was accentuated by the frame of his rectangular glasses. Before she could sit, he beckoned Ava with a finger. She nodded and entered, taking a seat on the available chair inside.

Ava smoothed the creases in her slacks and readjusted her matching blazer.

"I'm Greg Carlin. You're Ava, right?"

She nodded. "Yes, sir. Ava Quinn."

He pulled the copy of her resume up on his monitor and glanced over it. "Burton Laboratories… Chief Revenue Officer… wow, over nine years."

Ava plastered on a smile and nodded. "Yes, sir. I moved up the ranks. I was promoted to that position about three years in."

"So what does a job like that entail, exactly?" He wove his fingers together on his lap and rocked back in his seat.

"Over the years, I did a little bit of everything in the finance department. It shrunk down, and then it grew so fast that I was doing the jobs of at least three separate positions. Over the last decade, the company had grown from mid-size to a larger enterprise, grossing roughly seven billion annually. So, I provided all the financial information for smaller proposals, put together forecasts, and did cost analysis. I oversaw corporate takeovers. And, eventually, acquisitions is where I really flourished."

"I see." His chair groaned as he leaned forward. "This position is for our Finance Director. We want someone who can help us formulate strategies, oversee budget planning, and supervise compliance. Does this sound like something you could do?"

"Yes, sir, absolutely."

"You seem pretty confident about that." He smiled.

"Finance is the lifeblood of any large company. If you can't be confident in who's involved, then they have no business being there."

"Couldn't agree more. After all that *experience*, I'm surprised you'd be interested in a position at a smaller company like *Halafin*."

Oh God, please don't say it…

"Frankly, you seem… overqualified."

Mother fu—

Ava straightened her posture. "I've thought a lot about that recently. From your perspective, I see how I'd look like a bit of a flight risk, so to speak. With my degree and experience from such a massive company, it's understandable. But… I want you to think about this from *my* perspective, sir. I want a *change*. I loved what I did, but I hated never knowing the people around me. In retrospect, my last job seems like an endless sea of faces. I want to know the people that I work with. I want to celebrate office birthdays or comfort someone crying in the break room. I want to know the name of your *kid*." She gestured to the back of a picture frame facing away from her.

"Actually, I have two." He twisted it around on the desk. A smiling family stared back, and Ava felt a pang of sadness in her heart.

She would never have that. She would never even have the *next best thing*: a picture of her, Starla, and Will smiling on an outing together. As a *family*.

"...I want to be a part of something that needs me. I don't want to be one face in a million. I want to be one in twenty-five."

Mr. Carlin leaned back in his seat again. "You seem very passionate."

"I am, sir. I'm very passionate." *Sometimes too passionate,* she thought, recalling the look of horror on Will's face as he looked over her business proposal.

Mr. Carlin had all but said she was *overqualified.* If she was honest with herself, she didn't even really want the position.

She wanted to work with Will.

She wanted to be a part of building something amazing from the ground up, something she could nurture like a child out of its infancy until it could stand and walk on its own two legs.

Even if Will changed his mind, Ava knew there was a grain of truth to what he said.

The jealousy rocked her. There was a vulnerability in trusting someone who had the power to crush her. She'd already been broken and slowly mended the pieces. She didn't think she had the strength to be shattered like that again.

It was time to put away foolish thoughts of Will and *Man Maid*.

It was time for Ava to trudge forward into the future, even if it tore her apart to do it.

"I guess I just have one last question for you, Ava." Mr. Carlin smiled and put his hands behind his head. "When can you start?"

37

The waiting room of Dr. Harken's office had gotten upgraded with all new paint and furniture, and yet it was *still* as bland as a saltless cracker. The front desk beside them was void of any charming decor, not even displaying so much as a name tag. The assistant had stepped away to file something and had not yet returned. There were no magazines on the shiny new table in the waiting area. Everything was silent. The only sound was the swish of Starla's snow pants as she swung her legs in the chair beside him.

Through the deafening quiet, Will's head swam. He wished there was something — *anything* — to take his mind off of Ava. Staring forward at the plain beige wall before him was like gazing at a maddening image of his future.

Empty.

Dull.

His heart ached. The lump of emotion in his throat felt like he was swallowing a boulder.

"Dad, what's wrong," Starla asked sweetly, snow boots scraping the floor.

He was grateful for the interruption in his whirling thoughts. "Nothing, Honey." He forced a fake grin and wrapped his arm around her. "I always get a little anxious when they have to swap out your port."

Starla chuckled, smacking the heel of her boot with a thud against the carpet, watching packed squares of snow fall from it. "You're a bad liar."

"What?" He mustered a chuckle. "I'm not lying."

"Oh, puh-lease. Your voice always does this weird *thing* when you lie."

He laughed. "I'm not lying."

"*I'm not lying,*" Starla mimicked, her tone more like a cartoon version of Will's than anything. "And then you do that *throat* thing."

Will fought his desire to clear his throat and lowered his tone. "What are you talking about?"

Their heads turned as a baby mewled behind the exam room door. The muffled shushes of parents attempting to soothe the child followed.

"What are they doing in there?" Starla asked, shifting her attention.

Will, once again, welcomed the question. "Well, that baby is probably getting a vaccination. You used to scream like you were being *murdered*."

The very word murder *conjured memories of his date with Ava at the Million Dollar Cowboy Bar about serial killer documentaries. He wondered if she was watching one right now…*

Everything came back to Ava.

He couldn't shake her from his mind and, instead, pictured her there on the couch they'd nearly made love on. In his imagination, her shapely form was lounging comfortably in a baggy t-shirt and shorts, curvaceous legs draped across the dog as investigators in a cold case droned on.

The image overtook his thoughts. His chest throbbed at the loss of all that was, and all that certainly could've been.

Was she thinking of him, he wondered. *Or was she the type to never look back?*

He recalled the wedding photo he'd seen on her wall the day she came into his life, her hair perfectly pinned up in a messy bun, swirling tendrils pulled free. Thoughts of her green eyes stole the breath from his lungs. Her elegant neck was adorned with a delicate solitaire diamond perched at the base of her throat, the flesh a canvas he wanted to paint with lingering lip prints.

He thought about the other half of that picture, discarded in a landfill somewhere, never to be thought of again. She was fully capable of extricating things in life if they caused her pain.

Starla's small hand grasped Will's. His leg jiggled wildly, eyes snapping back to the floor. The short carpet was muddy with footprints large and small. He wished he had something - *anything* - to scrub out the mud. Maybe if he scrubbed hard enough, he could forget that he had botched things with the strongest, sexiest woman to ever walk into his life.

The door opened to the exam room, and a mother emerged, cooing to the crying infant against her chest. Glancing around, she did a double-take and smiled sheepishly when she spotted Will. Her makeup-free eyes were ringed in dark circles, most likely from sleep deprivation. She tucked a wild strand of frizzy hair behind her ear as she quickly made her way past him to the front desk.

Dr. Harken shuffled out to reception. The man was in his early sixties, sporting a head full of salt-and-pepper hair, narrow eyes, and a saggy neck. Today, against the drab walls of his office, the man looked a hundred. "Alright, Dana, it looks like we will submit this to your insurance right away. In the meantime, if little Liam here starts running a temp, won't eat, or has any signs of an allergic reaction, call me."

Dana nodded and readjusted the baby on her hip, jostling the diaper bag back on her shoulder. "Thank you. Have a good one." She gave a polite smile and turned toward Will.

He quickly glanced up at her face, another welcome distraction. She darted her eyes away nervously and hurried out of the clinic's front door.

"Why do ladies do that?" Starla asked her father quietly. "They always look nervous around you."

Will grinned. "I dunno, kiddo."

"They always look like they want to smooch you."

"Alright," Dr. Harken said, clapping his hands together. The startling noise bounced off the walls like a distant crack of thunder. "Who's ready to switch out their port?"

"He is," Starla joked, jabbing Will's down coat sleeve.

Dr. Harken chuckled. "Ah now, come on, Miss Starla. You and I had an agreement. We get this port in your tummy, and then you get two stickers of your choice."

"I see you finished the remodel. It looks nice," Will lied.

"Thanks! Yeah, it's nice to start fresh sometimes."

The words wrenched Will's gut. *Is that how Ava feels right now?*

As Will rose, he wondered if he could do the same... start fresh, knowing she was out there... probably thriving without him.

Will followed them into the exam room and shut the door.

"Now, Miss Starla, how have you been feeling? Any blood sugar dips?"

Will's eyes were locked on a painting hanging across the room, just beyond the examination table. It was a dreamy image of a mother and daughter holding hands with their feet in the water, small waves lapping at their legs.

It wasn't the image that caught his eye, but the brush strokes...

Small. Exact. Careful.

Not fluid, like a typical blended painting, but something more precise with hard lines and edges.

Will listened to the doctor ask Starla a myriad of questions, lost in thought, drawn to the painting on the otherwise bare wall. "Doctor, is that art new?"

"Huh?" Dr. Harken turned his head from the chart notes to follow his eyeline. "Oh! Yes, that was a donation from a lady here in town who paints 'em. I think they're those paint-by-numbers. You believe that? There's one in each of the exam rooms."

Will walked closer to the painting and viewed the signature at the bottom. Though the last name was a flurry of swirls, the first name was clear…

Ava.

Being this close to something Ava had spent so much time on made his heart ache. Each delicate shape of paint was met with the focus and precision of a surgeon, every boundary respected.

When she gave him that business plan, he pushed her away. And why?

For believing in him?

Even without sex, the intimacy was there, in the lines of her smile, in the feel of her body sleeping against his the night her ex had resurfaced.

He'd had lots of sex over the years, but never anything as intimate as that night with her. Just sleeping. Just holding her to his chest, legs intertwined. Until then, he hadn't known his life with Starla was missing anything important.

Now, he was painfully aware.

Starla hissed as Harken's age-spotted hand removed her port.

"You did great, sweetheart. You're getting to be an old pro at this," the doctor smiled.

"Those had better be *big* stickers." Starla grimaced.

"I just got some new ones in. You'll get the first pick."

"Alright, time for the new one, okay? Remember: deep breaths. Focus on wiggling your toes."

"Okay." Starla craned her neck toward the painting. "I like it, too."

"Yeah?" Will snickered, returning his eyes to the image once more.

Starla nodded and exhaled as the doctor skilfully installed the new device. Will grabbed Starla's small hand and kissed the top of her head.

***

Moments later, Will walked out of the doctor's office. "You sure you don't want me to carry it?"

"I got it, Dad. I have muscles. I can carry it."

"Yes," he chuckled, "you do have muscles."

Starla waddled to the car with the framed paint-by-number in her outstretched arms. He opened the back door and helped her lift it onto the floorboard in front of the bench seat. "Why did you buy this?"

"I liked it." He smiled. "I'm a fan of the artist."

"Now he doesn't have anything on his wall in there."

"Honey, for what we have paid him through the years for your diabetes stuff, he can afford something else to put on that wall." Will closed the door and made his way to the front. "Where do you think we should hang it?"

"At the house," she said looking down at the pug and princess sticker on her coat as she made her way to the passenger side.

"No-duh, smart-aleck. I meant, *where* in the house?"

She tiptoed to get the door open and struggled her way up into the seat like she was climbing a steep rock face. Will knew better than to try to help her. She always refused, insisting she wanted to get in on her own. "How about where that dumb *Cast-a-blanca* poster is in the living room?"

"Blasphemy!" Will's jaw hung open for a moment, appalled. "You know what? For *that*, you're grounded."

Starla giggled.

38

Ava's kitchen was already in disarray again. She wandered to the fridge and dragged it open. The only edible thing inside was leftover pizza, so she grabbed a slice and ate it cold. She wandered back to her bathroom, standing in front of the mirror long enough to feel uncomfortable. She stared at her puffy eyes and dark circles and made a face of mild disgust. She splashed water on her cheeks, dried it off, and applied a modest amount of makeup despite the fog of depression that seemed to bear down on her.

She was scheduled to start her new job in three days. *Why in the hell did she seem so miserable about it?*

Sifting through the clothes in her closet, she threw on some casual black leggings and an oversized charcoal sweater, ones that matched her mood.

Knock-knock.

Ava furrowed her brows and made her way to the door. She opened it, stopping cold when she realized…

It was Will.

The sight of him made her stomach somersault with nerves.

"Hey." Will leaned against the wooden railing of the front porch, hands in his pockets. A gray hoodie clung to his toned stomach, one nearly as tight as his dark jeans. "Look… I'm sorry."

"No, *I'm* sorry." Ava lowered her eyes to the ground and took a deep breath. "Want to come in?"

Will nodded and stepped inside, petting Kuda as he made his way to the couch.

The couch had memories, ghostly imprints in the fabric of their intimacy.

Kuda launched onto his lap and licked Will's face. "Oh, thank you, Kuda. That's so much love. *Who'sagoodboy*?"

The Pit Bull went wild from the affection, jumping off his lap and darting around the house at warp speed.

Ava smiled. "He's a goofy boy."

Will sighed deeply, unsure of where to start with a more in-depth apology.

" — I'm sorry I overstepped," Ava said instead. "I had good intentions, I promise. I just… I went overboard."

Will shook his head and buried the lower half of his face in his pressed hands. "No. You did something kind. I overreacted. The proposal… was a bit overwhelming, I'll be honest. But it's clear you're so good at what you do… *did*…"

"No. *Do*," she corrected. "Got hired this week."

"Wow, that's… fantastic. Congratulations." He didn't seem overjoyed by the news. He leaned back into the couch. Ava perched on the far end, sitting delicately on the edge of her seat. "What you proposed… a *franchise*… an incorporation… it's a massive commitment."

Ava scooted closer and placed her hand on his. "It is. I don't know what I was thinking. You have enough on your plate with a kid and your clients… in my head, it was more like a grand romantic gesture. I like you… a *lot*. I wanted to make your life better. Not *control* you or burden you."

"I know. I just lashed out because I didn't know how to feel about all of this. Plus, you offering to get involved... I've always heard horror stories about people who mix their work with their home life, and frankly, that scared the shit out of me, too. I like you a lot, too, Ava. You and me... *we* felt right to me. I didn't want to lose that if I could help it. Oh, the irony…"

"I can't promise that I won't ever feel jealous," she said. "If women are touching you, lusting after you, what's not to say after we fight one day that you don't give in to temptation?"

He grasped her hand tighter. "Ava, there has to be *trust*. I have not done anything except try to build that trust. I understand jealousy. I feel it sometimes, too. Hell, I felt it when your ex-husband was over here with his fucking *hands* all over you."

She nodded and rubbed her foot on the edge of the coffee table.

"Give me a chance to *prove* that I would *never* do anything like that to hurt you."

She smiled weakly, feeling a slight rush of hope and optimism that he was talking about their future.

"I want you back, Ava." He stared into her eyes with longing.

The words hit her like a tsunami, flooding her with a warm flood of joy.

"I miss you. I miss your *vivaciousness*. Your *energy*. Your kind nature. Your *body*... Jesus Christ." He bit his lip and studied her for a moment, locking every inch of her in his memory.

Ava smiled. "I want to be with *you*. I've missed you. Starla, too."

He laughed to himself quietly.

Ava grinned. "What? What's so funny?"

His eyes finally met hers. "You know we're *crazy* for doing this, right?"

"People get in relationships all the time—"

"I mean *Man Maid*. We are crazy for doing this, you and I. Starting a business together."

Ava gasped. "Are you saying… you are in?"

He nodded. "Oh, yeah. I'm in."

She fought the urge to scream, covering her mouth. "You aren't going to regret this!"

"Lately, I only seem to regret the things I *don't* do."

"Like what?" She grinned. "What do you regret not doing?"

Will smiled, leaned into her, and pressed his lips to hers. Ava melded against him as their tongues entwined. The kiss sent a bolt of arousing current down the length of her body.

He stripped off her sweater, pulling it over her head by the hem, auburn hair bouncing as it freed from the fabric. His eyes trailed from her neck to her breasts, ones hoisted up in a plum-colored bra. He tossed the sweater to the floor and traced his fingers down her neck, gliding it along the tops of her breasts before hooking his finger into the fabric between them. With a gentle tug, he pulled her closer to him.

Their lips melded, tongues softly caressing one another.

Ava reached for the zipper of his hoodie, gliding it down and shoving the fleece-lined fabric over his shoulders to expose the soft, gray t-shirt beneath.

Will struggled to free one of his arms from the sleeves, and they snickered against each other's lips.

She needed to feel his flesh on hers, their hearts pounding together with no barriers between them. She yanked at his shirt, eager to remove it. Will took it off in a swift motion, carelessly tossing behind the couch.

Their breathing hastened, each breath louder and more ragged. Sucking one of his lips between hers, she playfully nibbled.

Will pulled away and stared with a look of smoldering intensity that made her skin flush with warmth.

She wanted him.

Needed him.

Ava wasn't about to wait another minute. No interruptions, no delays. The world around them faded into obscurity, leaving only the two of them wrapped in a cocoon of desire, feeling the agonizing promise of satiation.

Will unclasped her bra and rubbed his hands across sacred skin. Skin that haunted him like an erotic slideshow ever since he'd tasted her against his front door. He ran his calloused fingers along the grooves the bra had left and pulled her closer.

But *close was not close enough.*

He wouldn't be satisfied until he was *inside of her*, feeling her slick warmth wrapped around him.

Absorbing the scene, he took a moment to appreciate the sexual deity awaiting him. Her heaving breasts in his face, stomach glistening with a sheen of sweat, inner thighs damp and warm.

She bit her lip with a look that begged all the cravings she'd utter if there were any breath left in her lungs.

He trailed kisses along her neck, drifting down, skimming lips along her tantalizing flesh before enveloping one of her pert nipples with his mouth.

She gasped, running hands through his hair and leaning into his lips. She felt lightheaded at the delicious warmth of his tongue against her skin, pelvis writhing against his growing erection with frantic anticipation.

He pulled his mouth away, giving her nipple one more playful lick before his hands shifted down. He gripped her ass tightly in both palms, aggressively pulling her hips closer to his cock, seeking the wetness between her pale thighs.

"*Fuck, I want you*," Will growled, lowering to his knees before her on the floor. She leaned back into the leather. He watched her for a moment. Breasts heaving, face flush.

Her look was a potent mixture of longing and lust, and he wanted to savor *every... fucking... second.*

He traced his hands across the top of the leggings, hooking his fingers into the waistband. She tipped her hips, and he pulled the stretchy fabric down her curves and tossed it to the floor. She stared down at him with a look of eagerness that sent blood rushing to his throbbing cock. Parting her legs with his hands, he trailed kisses up her thigh and dove deep, gliding his tongue up her sweet, wet slit.

Ava moaned as it explored her depths.

Slowly, agonizingly, he circled her clitoris, feeling her abdomen tighten beneath one palm and squeezing her breast with the other. Ava squirmed, drawing her legs up on the edge of the couch, allowing him to go deeper. She dug her heels into the groaning leather.

Will voraciously lapped, savoring her taste, gently sliding a finger inside of her. She moaned as he slid in a second. His thumb massaged her sweet spot, making her buck from the sensation. She rubbed her fingers through his hair, silently begging for more with every sway of her hips.

Pleasure rocked through her body, sending a pulse of warmth through her like a hot flash. His skillful fingers coaxed her closer to the edge, suckling her through euphoric growls.

Her moans only drove him to want to please her more.

Her body quaked with an orgasmic shudder. She cried out into the air, pelvis pulsating around the slow withdrawal of his fingers.

"*Fuck me*," she panted.

He locked eyes with her, licking the wetness from his lips. "*Beg for it.*"

"*I want you inside of me.*" She squirmed, aching for him, eyes fluttering with an aftershock from her climax. "*Please,*" her breathy word was drawn out as she pleaded.

A look of pure excitement flashed across his blue eyes. Without another word, his jeans and briefs were shed, abandoned on the carpet near hers. He rose, abs flexed, muscles taut.

Ava couldn't take her eyes off his thick cock, which stood rod-straight, aggressively sprung to attention. The rumors she'd heard had proved true about him, and Ava had met her match.

She leaned forward and took him into her mouth, slow and deep, feeling him in the back of her throat as Will stroked her hair lovingly. His head laid back limply. His mouth opened in a silent gasp as she swirled her tongue along his firm crown and hard shaft.

It felt like bliss.

She glanced up at him, eyes moss-green and full of lust, saying far more than her mouth ever could if they were not already occupied. She savored his taste, taking him so deep into her throat that he groaned.

Will pulled her back gently by the hair, dick sliding from her heavenly lips. He crawled on top of her like a stalking lion, never blinking, ready to prey.

His heart was beating a mile a minute, reminding him just how alive they were.

But, gazing into her eyes, it all felt so different. Deeper…

This wasn't *just sex*. This was something *more*. Something that went far beyond flesh against flesh. There was *care*. There were *feelings*, ones that heightened the sensation to a level he'd never yet experienced with other women.

Ava mewled as Will slid inside of her.

His head rushed from the long-awaited sensation of her tight, pulsing walls flexing around his girth.

She turned her head, groaning into the leather as his thickness filled her, plunging slow and deep.

He felt her tremble against him, face contorted. She rocked her pelvis against him slowly, back arching, breasts in the air, moaning from the friction.

He thrust hard and deep, burying himself deep inside of her. It was a feeling he never wanted to end. He leaned down to kiss her, dick throbbing inside of her hot wet warmth. He gazed into her eyes, caressing the side of her face for a moment before sliding himself in deep again.

"*Fuck,*" he whispered into her ear. His gruff tone was enough to tip her over the edge of no return a second time.

At that moment, she knew she could never go back to the way life was before meeting Will Jessup.

His body savored every ounce of her pleasure as she trembled beneath him.

As the crashing waves of her orgasm simmered, she looked up. His brilliant blue orbs soaked in every bit of her. She wrapped her legs around his hips.

His thrusts quickened. It took every ounce of restraint he could muster to focus on something else, *anything* else, other than the orgasm building inside him. He bit his lip hard to redirect his mind as her moans grew louder. The feel of her nails dragging across his back spurred his pleasured body to release.

Some feral part of himself urged him to bury himself inside of her and come undone. His body expertly worked to stroke every sensitive spot. It made Ava's heart pound against his own.

His thrusts grew fevered, gaze steely. His nearing orgasm made her body grip him harder. As Will's cock pulsed, Ava savored the feel of him finishing inside of her in the most intimate display of trust she could fathom. Their bodies melded into one sweat-beaded form on the couch. Absorbing the sight of her, Will couldn't speak. She was breathtaking, dewy, and radiant with an otherworldly air of beauty.

This woman was a dream come true.

He nestled into the too-small nook of the couch beside her and scooped her in his arms. He lay there for a while, clutching her tight, savoring the warmth of her China-smooth skin.

A sense of peace washed over them both. Soon, Ava was asleep, naked in his loving arms.

39

"Can you put a little more oil on those abs, Ava? Just apply it off to the side there so you don't get it on the endless," ordered the photographer.

Will stepped to the side of a draped paper backdrop in a studio full of hung lights and flags placed just so on C-stands.

"Yes, no problem, Scooter."

"*Scooter*?" Will whispered as he approached. "You hired a guy named *Scooter* to do the shoot?"

Ava giggled and doused her hands in baby oil, sliding them along every nook and cranny of Will's chest with a shit-eating grin.

"Stop, Ave. You're gonna give me a hard-on," he grumbled. "Second one today." He winked, thinking back to their morning glory.

"Would that be such a crime? Those goods would only help us sell this service, baby."

"What am I doing? I'm not a *model*. We should've gotten some other guy to do this shoot. I got *no idea* what I'm doin'."

"It's all good. Barrett is coming in in twenty minutes to do his sexy courthouse judge shoot for the other promo. Then, Kerry is coming to play a naughty fire chief at three."

Will shook his head, fighting a smile. "This is so wild."

Ava looked up into his eyes, tone soft and comforting. "You are the sexiest man I have *ever* met. This is for *Man Maid*. Let's sell these rich ol' ladies the *dream*. You got this." She wiped her hands on a towel and smiled.

"*You owe me later.*" He winked.

"Deal." Ava slapped his ass as he walked away.

Will laughed and took his place on the endless backdrop again. In the bright lights, his body glistened.

Ava turned back to the photographer and gave him a thumbs up. "All good, Scooter."

"Thank you." Scooter changed his aperture, focused his lens, and started clicking off shots. Images appeared on the open laptop nearby tethered to the DSLR with a long wire. With short, shuffling steps, he went to the edge of the backdrop and tugged out a light meter from his back pocket. He held it up in front of Will's face and then in front of the crotch of his yellow briefs, ones that matched the shade of the yellow dish gloves his rippled arms were bursting out of.

"Mr. Jessup, it's showtime."

"*Alright, Mr. DeMille. I'm ready for my close-up*," Will said, doing his best impression of the character from Sunset Boulevard.

"How about you hold up the spray bottle this time?"

Ava scurried over with it, wiped the unbranded bottle clean with a rag, and handed it to Will. He held it near the center of his chest.

"Like this?"

"Do we still need the cleaning gloves? My hands are getting sweaty in these."

"*Yes*," Ava and Scooter said in unison.

They looked at each other, and Ava smiled sheepishly.

"Who's shoot is this?" Scooter snarled, at least a foot shorter than she was in her heels. "Who's behind the camera?"

"You are," Ava said quietly.

"Yes. So *please* let me work." Scooter turned back to Will and looked through the eyepiece. "Little to the right, Mr. Jessup."

Will took a half-step to the right.

"No. Turn your *body* to the right!" The man's short fuse made Will twist his face for a moment.

Will stepped back into position and turned his body slightly.

"There you go. Now, turn your face more to the right."

Will obliged, eyes wide with uncertainty.

"Will, you look like you're being held hostage. How about you soften those eyes and give us a grin?"

Ava's sympathetic expression turned into a mischievous grin. She could mess with Will, and all he could do was *watch*.

Ava took two steps straight back, feet behind the photographer, who was engrossed in his work. She peered around to make sure there were no extra prying eyes she'd missed.

Will watched, unmoving, as she unbuttoned the top three buttons of her silk blouse. She sat in a folding chair further back and leaned forward, pressing her curvaceous breasts together with her arms, allowing her buttoned-down shirt to flare open for a spectacular show of cleavage.

Will's eyes drifted down to her breasts, and he bit his lip to keep from smiling.

The photographer's voice was muffled from behind the camera. "Good. The lip bite is good."

Ava took her index finger and eased it into her mouth. She closed her eyes and pretended she was giving Will a blowjob, pulling it out and pushing it in deep and slow, eyes closed with pleasure.

Oblivious to her raunchy display, the photographer continued. "Alright, Will. Bite a little less. It looks like you are about to draw blood. Just let your face go slack."

Ava slid her slick finger down her chin and her neck, angling it down between her breasts, pressing it down through her cleavage.

Will's eyes were locked on her, and he felt his dick begin to stiffen.

This was about to be *very* awkward…

Will's eyes begged for her to stop.

A wide, devious smile spread across Ava's face as she removed her hand from her shirt, trailed it down her stomach, and stopped at the hem of her skirt. She leaned back and spread her legs towards him, rubbing herself beneath the fabric.

"Now tilt your chin up like you are looking toward a brighter future," Scooter ordered.

Will reluctantly lifted his chin up, eyes straining to stay locked on Ava.

"What are your eyes doing? Look up, Will."

Will did as he was told, taking in a deep breath, gripping the yellow bottle of fluid in his hands too tightly.

Ava snickered, buttoning back up her shirt and lowering her skirt with a devious smile.

"Okay, I think I can work with that. We've got you some good shots." Scooter nodded back at Ava. "I think you'll like these. Give me a few days, and I will have these over to you. I'm going to prepare for the next model. Will, you can get cleaned up."

As the photographer backed away, he finally noticed the bulge in Will's underwear. Without a word, he powered off his camera and pointed to it. "If we could show *that* on a billboard, I think your client list would skyrocket."

"T-thank you." Will shook his head, trying not to laugh at how bizarre life was sometimes.

Ava grabbed Will's hand and led him out of the studio into the vacant stairwell. There, he pushed her up against a wall and held his lips merely an inch from hers. "You played dirty in there."

Ava nodded proudly.

Will kissed her, running his fingers up the sides of her face and into her hair, bringing her closer as his roaming tongue conveyed the lustful thoughts he felt.

Ava tilted her hips toward his and turned her face away from him. "I don't play fair. And let's be real… you don't *want* me to."

Will turned her face back to his, hiked up her skirt, and pressed his oiled body between her thighs.

"You're right. But I don't play fair either." He dragged his lips against her neck.

A surge of warmth rippled through Ava's body.

"Say you *want me*... and you can *have me*."

Ava's cheeks flashed red with lust. "I'll make *you* cave first." She plunged her oiled hand down the front of his underwear and wrapped her fingers around his dick.

He growled in her ear and rubbed her clit through the fabric of her panties. Breath caught in her throat, and she let out a small, involuntary moan. Ava's eyes pinched shut, feeling her defiance melt away with every small circle his fingertip rubbed.

"I..." She began, breath hitching.

Suddenly, a throat cleared beside them. Ava jerked her hand out of Will's pants, and Will backed away, trying -- *and failing* -- to look casual.

Scooter held up a gray, ribbed tank top and a pair of shorts. "You, uh, forgot this."

Will took it from his hand, throwing the shirt on inside out and backward. The photographer left, closing the stairwell door behind him.

Ava and Will giggled all the way back to Will's pickup truck outside. They threw open the doors to the back seat and hopped inside.

Crashing into one another in a fevered frenzy, Ava and Will hungrily tore at each other's clothes.

Will plunged his hand beneath her underwear, feeling himself harden to a painful level at how wet she was.

Ava grabbed Will's shaft and rubbed, coaxing a groan from her handsome lover.

"Just say it," Ava whispered against Will's mouth. "*Just say you want to fuck me first, and I'll give you what you want.*"

Will moaned as her slick hand pumped faster. He pulled her hand away, forced his underwear and shorts onto the floorboard, ripped off Ava's panties, and rumpled her skirt up around her waist.

Ava spread her legs and shook her head, aching vagina on full, beautiful display. Milk white skin with a tuft of auburn hair around a rosy vulva.

Will was dying to be in her.

He stroked himself, soaking in the sight of her as she giggled.

"All you have to do is say the words. Give in." She smiled playfully. "You know you *want* to."

Without so much as a smile, Will stared at her for a moment, sweeping a thick chunk of red-brown hair from her face. "I love you."

Her smile froze for a moment and then fell. She felt like her heart was in her throat.

"That wasn't what—"

"I know," he laughed, eyes bouncing to the floorboard and then back to her. "I just wanted you to know that."

Ava stared at him for a long time before speaking.

"I love you, too."

His fingertips caressed her bare thighs for a few seconds.

Ava leaned forward to kiss him, wrapping her arms around his shoulders and pulling him back until he was on top of her.

Slowly, Will pressed himself into her, working his way slowly up to steady, fevered strokes. Ava moaned, throwing her head back against the window.

For the next hour, Will expressed his gratitude for Ava's sultry display in the studio…

Several times.

40

"That's a big damn sign," Will said, staring up at a billboard plastered with his muscular chest, gloved hands holding a bottle of cleaning fluid. The words *Man Maid, Inc.* were bright and bold across it, screaming out for attention in an embarrassingly affluent part of their small, mountain town.

Months had passed. The enterprise had been established. The paperwork was filed. The company was incorporated. Every "I" dotted and "T" crossed.

Now, they hoped their marketing campaign would start to pay its dividends.

"You really think this is gonna work?" Will asked.

"It's going to work. These upper-class men are gonna hate having this here. Hell, they might even make us take it down. But in the meantime, their wives will see it. This thing will do its job." Ava smiled proudly and put her hands on her hips. "We cast out our bait. Now we just gotta wait for the nibbles."

Ava's cell phone rang as if on cue. She glanced at the unfamiliar number and answered it, mustering her best impression of a professional receptionist.

"*Man Maid Incorporated.*" She smiled at Will and then looked up at the forty-foot six-pack of abs perched near the highway. "This is Ava. How can I help you?"

Epilogue

"Can I take off the blindfold now? What's with all the secrecy?"

Ava felt the rental car come to a full stop and heard Will kill the engine.

"You'll find out here in a minute."

The sound of wobbling poster board flapped. Ava could feel the gentle breeze of it on her skin along with the setting afternoon sun through the window.

"Stay here in the car for a second, okay?" Will murmured.

Ava nodded, tempted to peek, torn by her love of surprises. As the car doors opened and shut, she decided it best to keep the fabric on.

Faint whispers chattered outside, followed by scrambling footsteps in powder and the shuffle of the boards.

The door clicked open again, and she felt Will's hand slip into hers. "Alright, honey, you gotta step down gently. You're going to feel grass beneath your feet, not snow, okay?"

Ava laughed. This all felt ridiculous. "What is going on?"

She felt him gently press his lips to hers for a soft kiss. "You'll see soon enough."

Ava let Will lead her out of the car and ten feet further through the frozen grass. She heard Starla, unable to control her chipmunk-like giggles.

"Stay here, okay? I'll tell you when to take the blindfold off."

"Seriously, guys! What's going on?" Ava bobbed like she had to pee.

"It's a surprise," Starla shouted.

She could hear Starla and Will whisper to each other for a moment and then come to some sort of agreement.

Then, Will's voice. "You can take it off now."

Ava pulled the blindfold off, stunned by her surroundings.

She was in a vibrant cherry orchard. Mountains sat in the distance behind a valley of budding greenery. Hundreds of cherry trees over vast Oregon acreage rained down like pink-and-white snow behind Will and Starla.

Ava clasped her hands around her face, eyes welling with tears.

"We know you love cherry blossoms, so when I found out about this orchard, I *had* to take you."

It was only then that Ava realized Will and Starla were concealing something behind their backs. Will nudged his daughter with his shoulder. "Go."

Starla held up a ten-by-ten piece of poster board with the word WILL drawn in marker on it. She held up a second, which said YOU in bold black.

Will smiled, eyes glistening, and held up a piece that said MARRY, followed quickly by another that said ME?

Will. You. Marry. Me?

Tears escaped Ava's green eyes, dribbling down her cheeks in streams of elation.

"Well?" Will asked, handing the pieces to Starla and approaching Ava. He dropped to one knee and pulled a ring box out of his pocket, opening it before her. A diamond ring, tasteful and elegant, sat tucked in the black velvet. "Will you marry me?"

Ava nodded, tears flowing freely. "Yes."

Will placed the ring on her finger and kissed her.

"She said yes, Star!"

Starla rejoiced, racing up to Ava and wrapping her legs in a tight hug. In this perfect moment, surrounded by the rain of petals, Ava felt, for the first time, that she truly had a family of her own.

About the Author

Aurora Alba is a writer of contemporary romance, paranormal romance, fantasy, and mystery.

She hails from a small town in Wyoming and writes with the full support of her husband and fur-babies. She strives to be a captivating storyteller. Love, in all forms, is her passion.

Aurora has published books in fantasy under her real name, Heather Wohl, and horror as H.M. Wohl.

A Note From The Ogres

Even though this book was proofread thoroughly by professionals, beta readers, and ARC readers… mistakes happen. We want our readers to have the best experience possible. If you spot any spelling, grammatical, or formatting errors, please feel free to reach out to us at:

Rustyogrepublishing@gmail.com

Reviews

If you could take the time to leave an honest review after you've read this book, we would greatly appreciate it. We respect your time and promise it doesn't *have* to be long and eloquent. Even a few words will do!

As a small publishing house, every review helps others determine if this book is right for them and greatly increases our chances of being discovered by someone else who might enjoy it.

The
Billionaire's
Assistant
Odessa Alba
A NEW ENGLAND BILLIONAIRES BOOK

The Billionaire's Assistant

Book one of the New England Billionaire's Series. Available worldwide in ebook, paperback, hardcover. Audiobook releasing in May of 2024.

Welcome to New England, home of scenic beaches, dazzling autumn foliage, and swoon-worthy affluent billionaires. Hindered by a broken arm, Eric Salko's life is upended when the VP of his investment firm, Rob, hires him a temporary new personal assistant. The moment the stunning employee enters his palatial Greenwich, Connecticut estate, all bets are off.

With her life in shambles, Kira Blumquist is desperate to make the most of her lucky break, but the growing attraction to her new boss threatens to jeopardize everything. Like a moth to a flame, she soon secretly finds herself yearning for his forbidden touch.

Odessa Alba's sensual series debut sizzles with smoldering heat, opulence, and a heartwarming HEA.

The Ugly Sweater
PARTY
A FORCED PROXIMITY ROMANCE NOVELLA
AURORA ALBA &
ODESSA ALBA

The Ugly Sweater Party

By Aurora Alba & Odessa Alba

Available in paperback, ebook, & audiobook.

Ascending to a holiday party on the thirty-second floor of a Manhattan skyscraper, the building's only elevator breaks down, trapping grinchy curmudgeon "Nasty Nate" DuPont and the stubborn Director of Finance, Twila Henderson, inside. With bumbling maintenance workers en route and emotions running high, Twila and Nate struggle to stay civil. As hideously dressed co-workers mingle feet beyond their blocked exit, stuffed emotions bubble to the surface over the captive duo's seemingly forgotten past.

Bursting with heat and humor, this third-person steamy laugh-riot will leave you with an HFN that will warm your heart on even the coldest winter night. From the Alba sisters (authors of *The Billionaire's Assistant* & *Call of the Wyl*) comes a spicy standalone contemporary romance novella for fans of forced proximity, enemies-to-lovers, workplace romance, grumpy boss, holiday romance, & romantic comedy tropes.

Call
of
the
Wyl
A DESTORIAN ADVENTURE NOVELLA
Heather Wohl

Call of the Wyl

A Standalone Destorian Fantasy Novella with a dash of paranormal romance

Available worldwide in ebook and audiobook

What would it take to send your own brother to the dungeons?

Wyl bounty hunter, Brutus, is in hot pursuit of his elusive brother, Otis. With a bounty on his sibling's head (and Brutus in desperate need of fast coin) he must bring his own relative to justice. Along his mysterious journey, Brutus finds himself in the clutches of Brute Fest, a violent festival where black eyes and vicious brawls are celebrated. His trip takes an even more intriguing turn when he becomes enraptured by a rose-gold beauty named Violet. Captivated by the wild, new world around him, Brutus must make an impossible choice between love, money... and family.

Coming Soon!

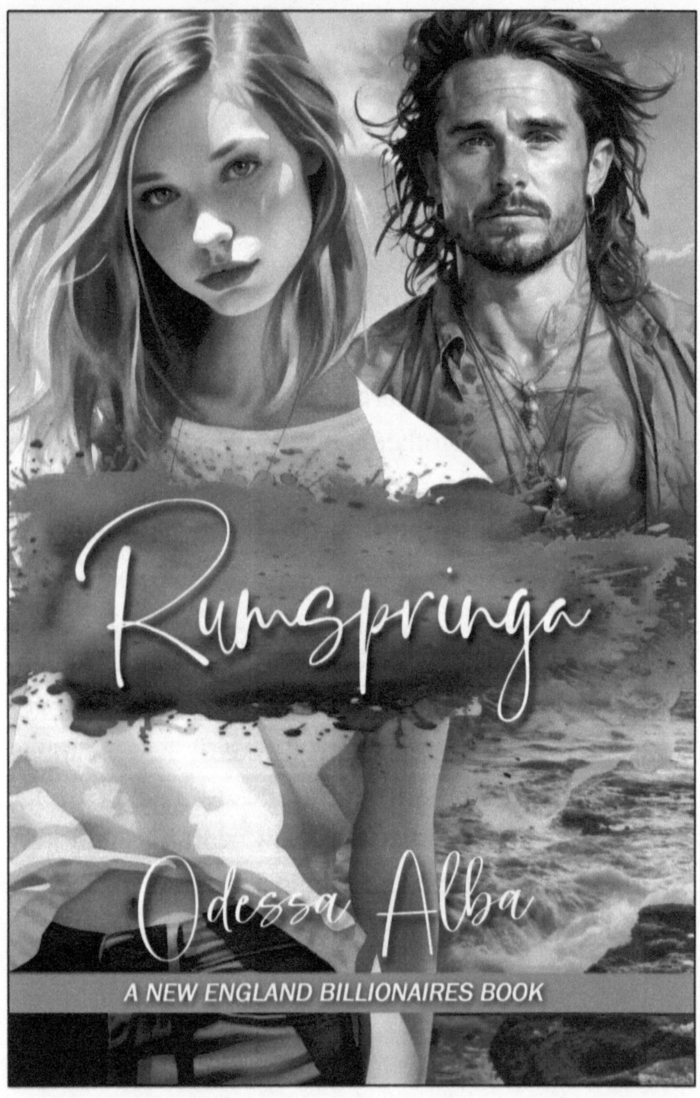

Rumspringa
Odessa Alba
A NEW ENGLAND BILLIONAIRES BOOK

Maid
in America
BOOK TWO OF THE MAN MAID SERIES
AURORA ALBA

www.ingramcontent.com/pod-product-compliance
Lightning Source LLC
Chambersburg PA
CBHW020229010826
48973CB00006B/1438